W9-BRD-068

KNOW YOUR GOVERNMENT

How Laws Are Passed

The Constitution
The Democratic Party
The House of Representatives
How Laws Are Passed
How the President Is Elected
Impeachment
The Presidency
The Republican Party
The Senate
The Supreme Court

KNOW YOUR GOVERNMENT

How Laws Are Passed

By Justine Rubinstein

MASON CREST
PHILADELPHIA • MIAMI

Mason Crest
450 Parkway Drive, Suite D
Broomall, Pennsylvania 19008
(866) MCP-BOOK (toll-free)
www.masoncrest.com

Printed in the United States of America

First printing
9 8 7 6 5 4 3 2 1

Series ISBN: 978-1-4222-4231-5
Hardcover ISBN: 978-1-4222-4235-3

Cataloging-in-Publication Data is available on file at the Library of Congress.

Developed and Produced by Print Matters Productions, Inc.
(www.printmattersinc.com)
Cover and Interior Design by Lori S. Malkin Design, LLC

QR CODES AND LINKS TO THIRD-PARTY CONTENT:

You may gain access to certain third-party content ("third-party sites") by scanning and using the QR Codes that appear in this publication (the "QR Codes"). We do not operate or control in any respect any information, products or services on such third-party sites linked to by us via the QR Codes included in this publication, and we assume no responsibility for any materials you may access using the QR Codes. Your use of the QR Codes may be subject to terms, limitations, or restrictions set forth in the applicable terms of use or otherwise established by the owners of the third-party sites. Our linking to such third-party sites via the QR Codes does not imply an endorsement or sponsorship of such third-party sites, or the information, products, or services offered on or through the third-party sites, nor does it imply an endorsement or sponsorship of this publication by the owners of such third-party sites.

CONTENTS

INTRODUCTION: The Evolving American Experiment 6

Chapter 1 ★ How Congress Is Organized 10

Chapter 2 ★ Introducing New Legislation 22

Chapter 3 ★ Consideration by Committee 34

Chapter 4 ★ Initial House Action 44

Chapter 5 ★ Senate Review 54

Chapter 6 ★ Final Congressional Approval 64

Chapter 7 ★ Presidential Action 76

SERIES GLOSSARY OF KEY TERMS 88

FURTHER READING & INTERNET RESOURCES 92

INDEX 95

CREDITS 96

Key Icons to Look For

Words to Understand: These words with their easy-to-understand definitions will increase readers' understanding of the text while building vocabulary skills.

Sidebars: This boxed material within the main text allows readers to build knowledge, gain insights, explore possibilities, and broaden their perspectives by weaving together additional information to provide realistic and holistic perspectives.

Educational Videos: Readers can view videos by scanning our QR codes, providing them with additional educational content to supplement the text.

Text-Dependent Questions: These questions send the reader back to the text for more careful attention to the evidence presented there.

Research Projects: Readers are pointed toward areas of further inquiry connected to each chapter. Suggestions are provided for projects that encourage deeper research and analysis.

Series Glossary of Key Terms: This back-of-the-book glossary contains terminology used throughout this series. Words found here increase the reader's ability to read and comprehend higher-level books and articles in this field.

The Evolving American Experiment

From the start, Americans have regarded their government with a mixture of reliance and mistrust. The men who founded the republic did not doubt the indispensability of government. "If men were angels," observed the 51st *Federalist Paper*, "no government would be necessary." But men are not angels. Because human beings are subject to wicked as well as to noble impulses, government was deemed essential to ensure freedom and order.

At the same time, the American revolutionaries knew that government could also become a source of injury and oppression. The men who gathered in Philadelphia in 1787 to write the Constitution therefore had two purposes in mind. They wanted to establish a strong central authority and to limit that central authority's capacity to abuse its power.

To prevent the abuse of power, the Founding Fathers wrote two basic principles into the new Constitution. The principle of federalism divided power between the state governments and the central authority. The principle of the separation of powers subdivided the central authority itself into three branches—the executive, the legislative, and the judiciary—so that "each may be a check on the other."

The Constitution did not plan the executive branch in any detail. After vesting the executive power in the president, it assumed the existence of "executive departments" without specifying what these departments should be. Congress began defining their functions in 1789 by creating the Departments of State, Treasury, and War. The secretaries in charge of these departments made up President Washington's first cabinet. Congress also provided for a legal officer, and President Washington soon invited the attorney general, as he was called, to attend cabinet meetings. As need required, Congress created more executive departments.

Setting up the cabinet was only the first step in organizing the American state. With almost no guidance from the Constitution, President Washington, seconded by Alexander Hamilton, his brilliant secretary of the treasury, equipped the infant republic with a working administrative structure. The Federalists believed in both executive energy and executive accountability and set high standards for public appointments. The Jeffersonian opposition had less faith in strong government and preferred local government to the central authority. But when Jefferson himself became president in 1801, although he set out to change the direction of policy, he found no reason to alter the framework the Federalists had erected.

The United States Constitution has been the supreme law of the United States since its signing in 1787. Its first three words, "We the People," affirm that the government is here to serve the people.

By 1801, there were about 3,000 federal civilian employees in a nation of a little more than 5 million people. Growth in territory and population steadily enlarged national responsibilities. Thirty years later, when Jackson was president, there were more than 11,000 government workers in a nation of 13 million. The federal establishment was increasing at a rate faster than the population.

Jackson's presidency brought significant changes in the federal service. Jackson believed that the executive branch contained too many officials who saw their jobs as "species of property" and as "a means of promoting individual interest." Against the idea of a permanent service based on life tenure, Jackson argued for the periodic redistribution of federal offices, contending that this was the democratic way and that official duties could be made "so plain and simple that men of intelligence may readily qualify themselves for their performance." He called this policy *rotation-in-office.* His opponents called it the *spoils system.*

In fact, partisan legend exaggerated the extent of Jackson's removals. More than 80 percent of federal officeholders retained their jobs. Jackson discharged no larger a proportion of government workers than Jefferson had done a generation earlier. But the rise in these years of mass political parties gave federal patronage new importance as a means of building the party and of rewarding activists. Jackson's successors were less restrained in the distribution of spoils. As the federal establishment grew—to nearly 40,000 by 1861—the politicization of the public service excited increasing concern.

After the Civil War, the spoils system became a major political issue. High-minded men condemned it as the root of all political evil. The spoilsmen, said the British commentator James Bryce, "have distorted and depraved the mechanism of politics." Patronage—giving jobs to unqualified, incompetent, and dishonest persons—lowered the standards of public service and nourished corrupt political machines. Office-seekers pursued presidents and cabinet secretaries without mercy. "Patronage," said Ulysses S. Grant after his presidency, "is the bane of the presidential office." "Every time I appoint someone to office," said another political leader, "I make a hundred enemies and one ingrate." George William Curtis, the president of the National Civil Service Reform League, summed up the indictment:

> The theory which perverts public trusts into party spoils, making public employment dependent upon personal favor and not on proved merit, necessarily ruins the self-respect of public employees, destroys the function of party in a republic, prostitutes elections into a desperate strife for personal profit, and degrades the national character by lowering the moral tone and standard of the country.

The object of civil service reform was to promote efficiency and honesty in the public service and to bring about the ethical regeneration of public life. In 1883, over bitter opposition from politicians, the reformers passed the Pendleton Act, establishing a bipartisan Civil Service Commission, competitive examinations, and appointment on merit. The Pendleton Act also gave the president authority to extend by executive order the number of "classified" jobs—that is, jobs subject to the merit system. The act applied initially only to about 14,000 of the more than 100,000 federal positions. But by the end of the nineteenth century, 40 percent of federal jobs had moved into the classified category.

The twentieth century saw a considerable expansion of the federal establishment. The Great Depression and the New Deal led the national government to take on a variety of new responsibilities. The New Deal extended the federal regulatory apparatus. By 1940, in a nation of 130 million people, the number of federal workers for the first time passed the 1 million mark. The Second World War brought federal civilian employment to 3.8 million in 1945. With peace, the federal establishment declined to around 2 million by 1950. Then growth resumed, reaching 2.8 million by the 1980s. In 2017, there were only 2.1 million federal civilian employees.

The New Deal years saw rising criticism of "big government" and "bureaucracy." Businessmen resented federal regulation. Conservatives worried about the impact of paternalistic government on individual self-reliance, on community responsibility, and on economic and personal freedom. The nation, in effect, renewed the old debate between Hamilton and Jefferson in the early republic.

Since the 1980s, with the presidency of Ronald Reagan, this debate has burst out with unusual intensity. According to conservatives, government intervention abridges liberty, stifles enterprise, and is inefficient, wasteful, and arbitrary. It disturbs the harmony of the self-adjusting market and creates worse troubles than it solves. "Get government off our backs," according to the popular cliché, and our problems will solve themselves. When government is necessary, let it be at the local level, close to the people.

In fact, for all the talk about the "swollen" and "bloated" bureaucracy, the federal establishment has not been growing as inexorably as many Americans seem to believe. In 1949, it consisted of 2.1 million people. Nearly 70 years later, while the country had grown by 177 million, the federal force is the same. Federal workers were a smaller percentage of the population in 2017 than they were in 1985, 1955, or 1940. The federal establishment, in short, has not kept pace with population growth. Moreover, national defense and security-related agencies account for nearly 70 percent of federal employment.

Why, then, the widespread idea about the remorseless growth of government? It is partly because in the 1960s, the national government assumed new and intrusive functions: affirmative action in civil rights, environmental protection, safety and health in the workplace, community organization, legal aid to the poor. Although this enlargement of the federal regulatory role was accompanied by marked growth in the size of government on all levels, the expansion has taken place primarily in state and local government. Whereas the federal force increased by only 27 percent in the 30 years after 1950, the state and local government forces increased by an astonishing 212 percent.

In general, Americans do not want less government. What they want is *more efficient* government. For a time in the 1970s, with the Vietnam War and Watergate, Americans lost confidence in the national government. In 1964, more than three-quarters of those polled had thought the national government could be trusted to do right most of the time. By 1980, only one-quarter was prepared to offer such trust. After reaching a three-decade high in the wake of the 9/11 terrorist attacks, public confidence in the federal government was near historic lows in 2017 at just 18 percent.

Two hundred years after the drafting of the Constitution, Americans still regard government with a mixture of reliance and mistrust—a good combination. Mistrust is the best way to keep government reliable. Informed criticism is the means of correcting governmental inefficiency, incompetence, and arbitrariness; that is, of best enabling government to play its essential role. For without government, we cannot attain the goals of the Founding Fathers. Without an understanding of government, we cannot have the informed criticism that makes government do the job right. It is the duty of every American citizen to know our government—which is what this series is all about.

How Congress Is Organized

Words to Understand

Apportion: The process of dividing something, such as money, amongst a group.

Biennial: Occurring once every other year.

Census: An official count of a population, often including other data or information about that population.

The United States federal government is made up of three unique branches: the executive, the legislative, and the judicial. Working together, the three branches form a powerful system for evolving our country's laws to meet new challenges while upholding the rights and responsibilities guaranteed by the U.S. Constitution. Working independently, no single branch is stronger than the other two, which ensures a balance of power and renders all three equally important. The core of the legislative branch of the U.S. federal government is called *Congress*. This is the branch responsible for introducing and preparing legislation that may become new law. Congress is supported by over a dozen agencies housed within the legislative branch, including the Library of Congress, the Congressional Research Service (CRS), the Government Accountability Office (GAO), and the Congressional Budget Office (CBO).

The diagram on the right breaks down what the party affiliations of the 115th Congress looked like. In the 2018 midterm elections, the Democratic Party took back control of the House.

UNITED STATES GOVERNMENT
115th CONGRESS

SENATE
100 MEMBERS

46 DEMOCRATS • 52 REPUBLICANS • 2 INDEPENDENTS

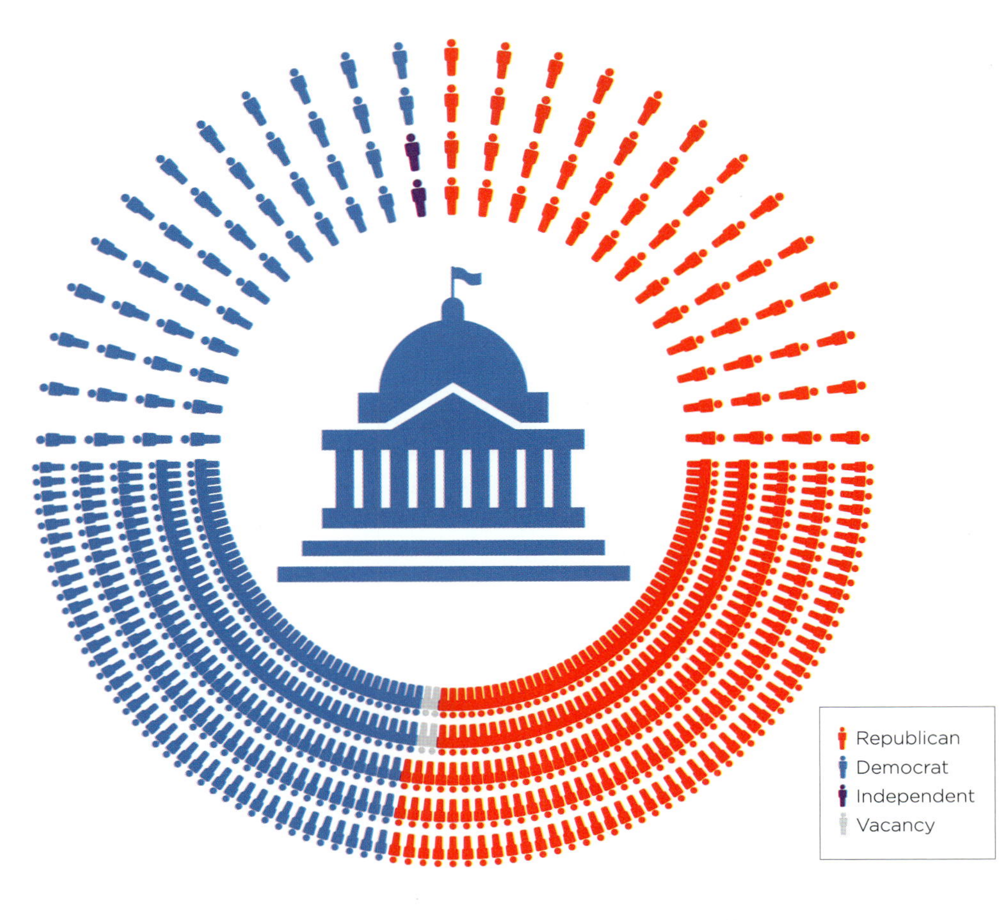

HOUSE OF REPRESENTATIVES
435 MEMBERS

193 DEMOCRATS • 238 REPUBLICANS • 4 VACANCIES

As established by Article I of the Constitution, Congress is divided into two distinct yet complementary parts: the House of Representatives, in which each member represents a relatively equal number of citizens; and the Senate, where delegates represent the entire state from which they are elected. Each body of Congress appoints its own leaders and functions by its own rules, but both play very similar roles in passing new legislation. The House and the Senate are further divided into committees, which provide expert focus on specific issues of proposed legislation prior to communicating to the entire Congress. This chapter provides an introduction to these key roles in the legislative process.

An overview of the legislative branch.

The House of Representatives

Truly the cornerstone of our democracy, the House of Representatives provides equal representation in Congress for every citizen of the United States, regardless of sex, race, economic status, or state of residence. The House of Representatives is made up of 435 members, each of whom represents an area of the country called a *congressional district*. The residents of a district choose the person they want to represent them in the House of Representatives by participating in general elections every two years. Once elected to Congress, representatives are the voices of their district residents, known as *constituents*, in the lawmaking process.

Every 10 years, the United States conducts a **census** to count its citizens. State governments then use population data generated by the census to redefine congressional districts, ensuring that each member represents a similar number of constituents. As a result, more populous states have more representatives in Congress. California, for example, has 53 districts based on 2010 census data of 37.3 million residents, whereas Idaho, with 1.6 million, has just two districts. Although a greater number of representatives does not necessarily translate to greater power for a state, crafty governors can redraw district boundaries to attempt to gain presence for their political parties in Congress.

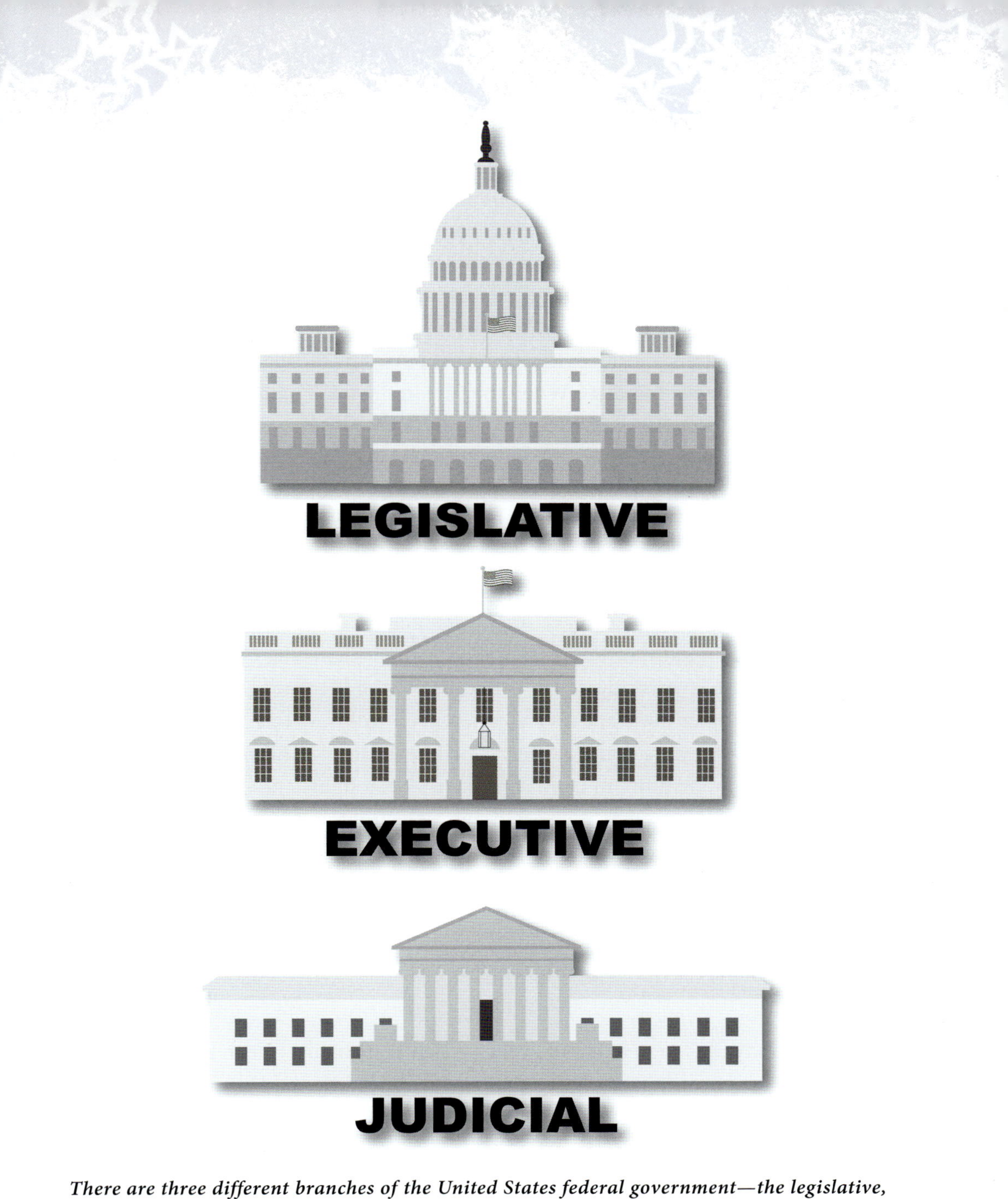

There are three different branches of the United States federal government—the legislative, executive, and judicial. Each of the three branches plays a specific role in the creation and maintenance of laws in the United States.

General elections occur on the first Tuesday after the first Monday in November during even-numbered years. On January 3 of the following year, the members of the House of Representatives convene in Washington, D.C., to begin the new congressional term. At the opening of a new term, representatives elect their House leader, known as the *Speaker*. The Speaker of the House is an incredibly powerful role because they influence many of the House committee assignments and determines the order in which the House addresses new legislation. The Speaker typically belongs to the House majority political party and often prioritizes legislation supported by the majority party over legislation endorsed by the minority. When they are in the same party, the Speaker of the House is the president of the United States' closest ally in all of Congress. When they are not, the Speaker can be the president's greatest political foe.

A term is divided into two year-long sessions. The chief function of Congress is to propose and pass legislation. The Constitution distinguishes the House from the Senate in this function, stating that only the House may propose legislation for raising and **apportioning** revenue. This refers to laws that increase taxes and to laws that determine how the government spends its money.

Through the House of Representatives, ordinary citizens can make a significant impact on the lawmaking process. Because of the **biennial** election cycle, representatives are under constant review. They need to know that their constituents approve of the job they are doing, so they welcome feedback. This provides interested citizens with an opportunity to communicate their thoughts and concerns to someone who actually votes on federal legislation in Washington, D.C., on a regular basis. Equally important is the ultimate tool of democracy—constituents have the power to vote their representative out of office in favor of another candidate who better represents their point of view.

The Senate

The second body of Congress is called the *Senate*. Its primary role in the lawmaking process is to review and improve legislation introduced by the House of Representatives. Representatives typically support legislation that addresses the immediate concerns of their constituents. Senators, who serve longer terms, and in most cases represent larger constituencies, often amend House-approved legislation to ensure that it is applicable to the broader public and will remain relevant over time. This system places the needs of the American people at the foundation of new legislation and at the same time leverages a long-term perspective to create better laws.

The Capitol Building in Washington, D.C., holds both houses of the U.S. Congress: the Senate and the House of Representatives. Each body has its own chamber, where full-membership official business is conducted.

Article I, Section 3, of the Constitution specifies that each state elect two members to the Senate, which provides each state with equal representation regardless of population. In 1959, Hawaii became the 50th state in the Union, which increased the number of members serving in the U.S. Senate to 100. Statewide constituencies vote for senators in the same general election process used to elect representatives. Because senators serve six-year terms, though, only about one-third of Senate seats are contested

THE TWO-PARTY SYSTEM

A person elected to serve in a government office, such as a senator or a representative, is called a *politician*. Political parties are groups of politicians who share a fundamental governing philosophy. For the most part, the U.S. government has always been a two-party system. Although the names of the parties have changed over the years, at any one time in our history, the vast majority of government officials have represented one of two parties. Today, the two major parties are the Democratic and Republican Parties. In the 115th Congress (2016–2020), zero representatives and only two senators represented a party other than Democratic or Republican.

The two-party system of the United States facilitates clear leadership in Congress—the political party with more seats leads. The majority party enjoys a variety of benefits: congressional leaders, such as the Speaker of the House and Senate majority leader, represent the majority party; majority party members are awarded the majority of committee seats; and all committee chairpersons belong to the majority party. Minority party members have little or no control over the legislative agenda. The Republican Party enjoyed a majority in the 115th Congress, winning 241 of 435 seats in the House of Representatives and 52 of 100 Senate seats.

during an election cycle. This system of staggered term expiration allows the Senate to function consistently and avoid any major disruptions in a single election year.

The vice president of the United States also serves as president of the Senate in what is recognized as largely a ceremonial role. The vice president rarely attends Senate debates and may vote on legislation only in the event of a tie; therefore, senators elect a president pro tempore ("temporary president") to lead in his absence. Generally, the president pro tempore is the most senior senator in the majority party, but the role is less powerful than Speaker of the House. In fact, the president pro tempore often delegates day-to-day leadership responsibilities to junior senators to get them accustomed to Senate procedures. The leader of the Senate on any given day is referred to as the *presiding officer*.

Real influence in the Senate exists not at the procedural level but along political party lines. Each party elects a floor leader, commonly referred to as the *majority*

The 100-member Senate meets to negotiate and debate new legislation, review proposals from the House, and carry out other official dealings in the Senate Chamber located within the Capitol Building.

leader (the leader of the party holding the majority of seats in the Senate) and the *minority leader* (the leader of the party in the minority), who represent their parties as both political strategists and party spokespersons. Although these roles are not defined in the Constitution, they have evolved over time to become essential to the lawmaking process. Similar to the Speaker of the House, the majority leader has emerged as the true leader of the Senate, wielding the power to set the legislative agenda, schedule debates and votes, and influence committee assignments.

Although the Senate and the House of Representatives are equal legislative partners, the Senate is often misconstrued as the upper house of Congress. The Founding Fathers contributed to this perception by establishing the Senate as the more mature and consistent house of Congress, with a higher minimum age requirement for senators and legislative procedures that remain constant from one election year to the next. Individually, senators wield more influence than representatives simply because they serve longer terms and are fewer in number (which enables them to sit on more committees), but in fact, neither body can perform its function without the support of the other.

Congressional Committees

New laws originate in the form of legislation called *bills*. During each term, thousands of bills are introduced to Congress on a range of topics concerning every facet of American life. In order to vote on these bills in a manner that represents their constituents, senators and representatives must fully understand the potential impact of each piece of legislation. Because of the large volume of these bills, it would be impossible for individual members of Congress to investigate each one, so Congress is divided into committees that study the legislation and draft reports. All congressional members may then use these reports to become properly educated and cast informed votes.

The vast majority of new bills are addressed by standing committees. These committees are formed at the start of a congressional term and remain in service throughout the term's duration. Congressional leaders categorize incoming legislation based on subject matter, and each category is under the jurisdiction of a standing committee. Any new legislation that falls under one of these predefined categories is assigned to the corresponding standing committee for initial examination.

If new legislation is introduced and it does not fall under the jurisdiction of a standing committee, Congress may establish a special (or "select") committee to address the bill. A special committee functions like a standing committee but disbands when its obligation is complete.

At the beginning of each new term, the Senate and the House vote on committee membership. Committee nominees are chosen by their floor leaders based on seniority and area of expertise. For example, the Committee on the Judiciary, which oversees the administration of justice, is composed primarily of lawyers. The majority party holds a majority of seats within a committee (except for the Select Committee on Ethics, which maintains an equal number of members from each party), and the most senior member of the majority party is typically named committee chairperson. The senior member of the minority party—called the *ranking member*—is second in command, but the chairperson controls the legislative agenda.

Standing and select committees are further divided into subcommittees for more focused investigation of legislation under a committee's jurisdiction. When a subcommittee completes its study, it reports its findings to the committee, which may then choose to present the bill to Congress for a vote.

The organization of Congress, as defined by the U.S. Constitution in 1787, continues to provide a framework for making laws in the twenty-first century. Congress has grown and expanded along with our country's population and the number of states, but its fundamental structure remains constant. When questions arise regarding the legislative process, Congress still turns to the Constitution for guidance and clarity.

The remainder of this book explains how federal laws are passed. The House of Representatives and the Senate are our country's federal lawmakers. Understanding their roles and organization is fundamental to comprehending the legislative process.

CONGRESSIONAL STANDING COMMITTEES

HOUSE OF REPRESENTATIVES	SENATE
Agriculture	Agriculture, Nutrition, and Forestry
Appropriations	Appropriations
Armed Services	Armed Services
Budget	Banking, Housing, and Urban Affairs
Education and Workforce	Budget
Energy and Commerce	Commerce, Science, and Transportation
Ethics	Energy and Natural Resources
Financial Services	Environment and Public Works
Foreign Affairs	Finance
Homeland Security	Foreign Relations
House Administration	Health, Education, Labor, and Pensions
Judiciary	Homeland Security and Governmental Affairs
Natural Resources	Judiciary
Oversight and Government Reform	Rules and Administration
Rules	Small Business and Entrepreneurship
Science, Space, and Technology	Veterans' Affairs
Small Business	
Transportation and Infrastructure	
Veterans' Affairs	
Ways and Means	

Each congressional committee has its own meeting room. Pictured here is the Committee on Ways and Means Hearing Room. This committee focuses on tax policy writing, and its members are not allowed to serve on any other committee. When Congressional committees are ready to bring their policies to the floor, they will hold a hearing. The hearing lets the committees collect information from experts and other policymakers.

EXAMPLES OF CONGRESSIONAL SUBCOMMITTEES

HOUSE OF REPRESENTATIVES	SENATE
Constitution and Civil Justice	Clean Air and Nuclear Safety
Workforce Protections	Rural Development and Energy
Digital Commerce and Consumer Protection	Children and Families
Energy and Mineral Resources	Privacy, Technology, and the Law
Coast Guard and Maritime Transportation	Health Care
Aviation	National Parks

Text-Dependent Questions

1. What are the three branches of the U.S. government?
2. Name one way the Constitution distinguishes the House from the Senate.
3. What is the primary legislative role of the Senate?

Research Project

Research one of the standing committees in the current Congress, of either the House or the Senate. Find out what the committee's focus is, its various subcommittees, its key members, and its recent legislative activity. Write a brief report summarizing your findings.

Introducing New Legislation

Words to Understand

Amend: To alter or change a text in some way.

Lobbyist: A person who advocates for particular policies or positions.

Preamble: An introductory statement.

Congress undertakes a wide variety of responsibilities in its service to the U.S. government and the citizens its members represent. As defined in Article I, Section 8, of the Constitution, congressional duties include establishing new post offices and federal courts (with the exception of the Supreme Court), supporting the armed forces, and declaring war. The Senate must approve all presidential cabinet nominees, but only the House may impeach the president. On top of these responsibilities, the primary function of Congress is to introduce legislation and prepare bills to become law. This chapter describes the first step in creating new laws.

A new law typically originates as a piece of legislation called a *bill*; however, it may instead take the form of a joint resolution. Joint resolutions

The Constitution was written in 1787, and since then, Congress has been the core of the legislative branch of our government, creating laws that affect our nation and people every day.

We the People of the United States, in Order to form a more perfect Union, establish Justice, insure domestic Tranquility, provide for the common defence, promote the general Welfare, and secure the Blessings of Liberty to ourselves and our Posterity, do ordain and establish this Constitution for the United States of America.

Article I

Article II

Article III

Article IV

Article V

Article VI

Article VII

The Word "the", being interlined between the seventh and eighth Lines of the first Page, The Word "Thirty" being partly written on an Erazure in the fifteenth Line of the first Page, The Words "is tried" being interlined between the thirty second and thirty third Lines of the first Page and the Word "the" being interlined between the forty third and forty fourth Lines of the second Page.

Attest William Jackson Secretary

done in Convention by the Unanimous Consent of the States present the Seventeenth Day of September in the Year of our Lord one thousand seven hundred and Eighty seven and of the Independance of the United States of America the Twelfth In witness whereof We have hereunto subscribed our Names,

do not only propose new laws; they also are used to advocate constitutional amendments and declare war. The legislative procedure to propose laws is identical for joint resolutions and bills, but joint resolutions include a **preamble**, or introduction, which communicates the importance of passing the new law. Because joint resolutions are far less common than bills, we refer only to bills throughout this book.

Origin of Legislation

Bills may be private or public. Private bills typically provide support to individuals and groups. Federal medical benefits and immigration rights are examples of provisions that originated as private bills. The majority of bills, however, are public bills, which address the general population. Just about anyone can draft legislation describing the need for a new law, and indeed, proposals for laws originate everywhere, from the president down to ordinary citizens. It is important to remember that politicians are in Congress to represent their constituents. If you have a good idea for a new law, then you, too, can get involved in the legislative process.

Although anyone can propose a bill, most bills originate from members of Congress. Congressional candidates commonly have ideas for laws to improve the lives of their fellow citizens even before they are elected to office. These ideas make up a candidate's platform, which he or she communicates to voters while campaigning. If the voting majority agrees with a candidate's platform, that candidate will likely be elected, putting him or her in a position to introduce the constituents' ideas to Congress. As a result, when the next congressional term commences, senators and representatives are already prepared to begin drafting bills on behalf of their constituents.

Other significant contributors of new legislation are **lobbyists**. Lobbying is the act of influencing lawmakers to support or reject legislation on behalf of interested parties. Special-interest groups, such as environmentalists and labor unions, often

"All the News That's Fit to Print"

The New York Times

LATE CITY EDITION

VOL. CXXIII . . . . No. 42,567

NEW YORK, SATURDAY, AUGUST 10, 1974

15 CENTS

FORD SWORN IN AS PRESIDENT; ASSERTS 'NIGHTMARE IS OVER'

Nixon Bids an Emotional Farewell to Washington

TEARS AT PARTING

Ex-President Warns Against Bitterness and Revenge

By JAMES T. WOOTEN

WASHINGTON, Aug. 9 — Richard M. Nixon, his face wet with tears, bade an emotional farewell to the remnants of his broken Administration today, urging its members to be proud of their record in government and warning them against bitterness, self-pity and revenge.

"Always remember, others may hate you," he told mem-

The text of Nixon's speech is printed on Page 4.

A Plea to Bind Up Watergate Wounds

By MARJORIE HUNTER

Special to The New York Times

WASHINGTON, Aug. 9—Gerald Rudolph Ford became the 38th President of the United States today, declaring that "our long national nightmare is over."

Calling upon the nation to "bind up the internal wounds of Watergate," he said, "Our Constitution works. Our great Republic is a government of laws and not of men. Here the people rule."

And then, his voice filled with emotion, he urged the nation to pray for his predecessor

The text of Ford's address will be found on Page 3.

and friend of a quarter century, Richard Milhous Nixon.

"May our former President, who brought peace to millions, find it for himself," he said.

Mr. Ford assumed the powers of the Presidency at 11:35 A.M., the moment that Mr. Nixon's letter of resignation was handed to Secretary of State

Constitution of the United States."

As the heavy applause ended, the 61-year-old President began perhaps the most moving speech of his career. Speaking in his flat Middle-western tone, but with what appeared to be a new sense of self-assurance, he said that he was assuming the Presidency under circumstances never before experienced by Americans.

Minds Are Troubled

"This is an hour of history that troubles our minds and hurts our hearts," he said.

"Therefore," he continued, "I feel it is my first duty to make an unprecedented compact with my countrymen. Not an inaugural address, not a fireside chat, not a campaign speech. Just a little straight talk among friends. I intend it to be the first of many."

Gerald R. Ford takes the Presidential oath, administered by Chief Justice Warren E. Burger. Mrs. Ford attends the White House ceremony.

G.M. to Raise Prices 9.5% On 1975 Cars and T...

PAPERS AND TAPES

Aide Doubtful That Ford Would Give Nixon Pardon

President Gerald Ford was sworn into office in the East Room of the White House following President Nixon's resignation in 1974. He immediately took occupancy of the Oval Office—the president's headquarters.

employ professional lobbyists who are experts in drafting legislation. Lobbyists may even provide research and resources to usher bills through Congress. Many former politicians become lobbyists as a way to utilize their legislative experience in the private sector. In an effort to limit the power of lobbyists, the government imposes strict guidelines preventing these groups from providing gifts to lawmakers in exchange for legislative support.

The president of the United States, too, has ideas for new laws, and some legislation originates from the Oval Office. Once a year, when the two houses of Congress

THE FORMAT OF A BILL

A bill drafted in the following format is ready for introduction to Congress:

"A BILL"

[One-sentence description here]

"Be it enacted by the Senate and House of Representatives of the United States of America in Congress assembled,"

[Full text of legislation here]

come together at the start of a new session, the president addresses the entire legislature and delivers the State of the Union address. In this speech, the president presents ideas for new legislation and follows up by submitting drafts of proposed bills to congressional leaders. During the remainder of the year, the president and other members of the executive branch may submit additional legislation to Congress to further their political agenda.

All proposed legislation eventually winds up on the desk of a senator or representative. When members of Congress receive bills originated by a third party, they may conduct additional research and **amend** the bills to ensure alignment with their platforms and the desires of their constituents. The final draft of every bill must be arranged in exactly the same way.

Introduction to Congress

Regardless of a bill's origin, whether it is from citizen, lobbyist, or president, only a senator or representative may introduce the new legislation to Congress. The member of Congress who introduces the bill can be as important as the legislation itself in determining its chances to become a law. Of the 10,078 bills introduced to the 114th Congress, only 329 were signed into law. A bill with local impact is best introduced by the representative of the affected district, but a member of the relevant committee (ideally, the chairperson of that committee) should sponsor a bill that has national influence.

The senator or representative who signs the bill and introduces it to Congress is known as the *primary sponsor*. In order to drive a bill to approval amidst the many thousands of other bills, the primary sponsor must increase awareness of the

RESIDENT COMMISSIONER AND DELEGATES

In addition to the 435 members of the House of Representatives who represent U.S. states and congressional districts, the House includes five non-voting delegates. Residents of the District of Columbia, American Samoa, Guam, the U.S. Virgin Islands, and Northern Mariana Islands are American citizens; therefore, they are eligible for representation in Congress. In addition, the Commonwealth of Puerto Rico elects a resident commissioner to the House of Representatives for a four-year term, and the five other territories elect delegates who each serve a two-year term. None of these territories has official representation in the Senate.

The resident commissioner and delegates are granted many, but not all, of the same rights as the official representatives. They may introduce bills to the House, serve on congressional committees, and vote on committee matters. However, the resident commissioner and delegates may not vote on matters presented on the floor of the House. As a result, although these representatives can play a part in drafting and reporting legislation, they do not have a voice in determining the final approval of a bill.

legislation. One way to do this is by enlisting the support of cosponsors. The majority rules in Congress, so the more members who support a bill, the better chance it has of approval. The primary sponsor often shares the bill with influential members of Congress in order to recruit original cosponsors, whose names will also be listed on the bill.

Once the new bill is properly formatted and sponsored, the process for introducing it to the House of Representatives is relatively simple. The House chamber features a wooden box called the *hopper*. To introduce a bill, the representative merely drops it into the hopper. The House clerk collects bills from the hopper and assigns each one a legislative number. House legislative numbers begin with "H.R.," to indicate that the bill originated in the House of Representatives, followed by a sequential numeral, such as "H.R. 6536."

The procedure is slightly different when introducing legislation to the Senate. Typically, the sponsoring senator hands the signed document to a Senate clerk. Because fewer bills originate in the Senate, however, senators may introduce the legislation formally by reading an accompanying statement declaring the merits of the bill. On presentation of a bill, fellow senators may object to its introduction. If this happens, introduction is postponed until the next day. A second objection would bump the bill to the Senate calendar to be addressed when the majority leader sees fit. Legislative numbers for bills introduced in the Senate begin with "S."

Above, then-Judge Sonia Sotomayor gives her testimony to the United States Senate Committee on the Judiciary on her nomination for the U.S. Supreme Court in 2009. Each Supreme Court nominee must be approved by a vote in the Senate.

With such a large number of bills introduced to Congress each year, similar legislation is inevitably submitted, either to a single chamber or to both the House and the Senate. Similar bills introduced concurrently to both bodies of Congress are called *companion bills*. They may be introduced coincidentally or as a tactic to increase the legislation's chances for approval. Similar bills introduced to one chamber of Congress are assigned to the same committee, where the redundancy is addressed. The committee may abandon one in favor of the other or draft an original bill based on the strongest components of each.

Committee Assignment

Combined across the House of Representatives and the Senate, Congress operates more than 30 committees and 200 subcommittees to manage its complex workload. Standing committees are established and their members are selected at the beginning of each new congressional term, which makes the process of assigning a bill to a committee highly predictable and relatively simple. Most bills introduced to Congress do not propose original ideas for new laws. Instead, they modify or amend existing legislation. Therefore, new bills are assigned to the committees that have dealt with related laws in the past. Once assignments are set, these bills are published and distributed to all members of Congress.

The *Congressional Record* is a continuous chronicle of all legislative action, including a verbatim account of Senate and House proceedings and committee meeting notes. Newly introduced bills, listed by their legislative numbers, appear in a section called the Daily Digest. Since 1873, the Government Printing Office has distributed the *Congressional Record* on a daily basis to members of Congress for use as a resource tool. All information contained in the document is a matter of public record. Today, the *Congressional Record* is publicly available on the Internet. Interested citizens can view the document on government Web sites and stay informed of congressional activities.

The chamber's presiding officer (either the Speaker of the House or the Senate president pro tempore) refers newly logged bills to their committee assignments. A complex bill may be assigned to multiple committees, each reporting on the portion of the bill under their jurisdiction. One committee must be designated the primary committee, however, and be responsible for the bill in its entirety. For example: An animal population–control bill assigned primarily to the House

Congressman Theodore G. Bilbo reads the Congressional Record *in March 1946. The* Record *is a chronicle of all legislative action, including accounts of Senate and House proceedings. It is distributed to members of Congress on a daily basis; it also can be accessed on the Internet.*

Committee on Agriculture, which covers animals and livestock, is also referred to the House Committee on Ways and Means because the bill establishes a special state-controlled fund.

A bill referred to committee becomes the responsibility of the committee chairperson, who adds the bill to the legislative calendar and prioritizes the list of bills on the calendar. The legislative calendar is the committee's to-do list. The legislative workload remains heavy at the committee and subcommittee levels, particularly

The first Speaker of the House was Frederick Muhlenberg in 1789. Since then, the Speaker of the House has changed over 60 times.

because members of Congress typically sit on multiple committees. As a result, some bills are never addressed at all. Because the chairperson always represents the majority party, this is the phase of the legislative process when the chamber's majority really begins to assert its power.

If a bill's sponsor does not believe that the committee chairperson is giving the legislation the attention it deserves, he or she may seek additional cosponsors to increase support for the bill. Other interested parties may get involved as well. Lobbyists, for example, often fund advertising campaigns to promote the benefits of a proposed law, and if the president supports the bill, he or she may communicate through the press the importance of quick approval. Engaged citizens may also follow a bill's progress. If they feel that their elected officials are representing their political parties rather than their constituents, then they, too, can get involved by organizing petition drives.

The three stages covered in this chapter—drafting legislation, introducing a new bill to congress, and referral to committee—are the main preparation steps in the legislative process. Once the committee chairperson adds a bill to the legislative calendar, the actual process of passing a law begins. This process was first documented in Thomas Jefferson's *A Manual of Parliamentary Practice*, which Jefferson compiled during his term as the second vice president of the United States (1797–1801) and published in 1812. In the following chapters, we will focus on a single bill and its path from committee through chamber approval to final signature.

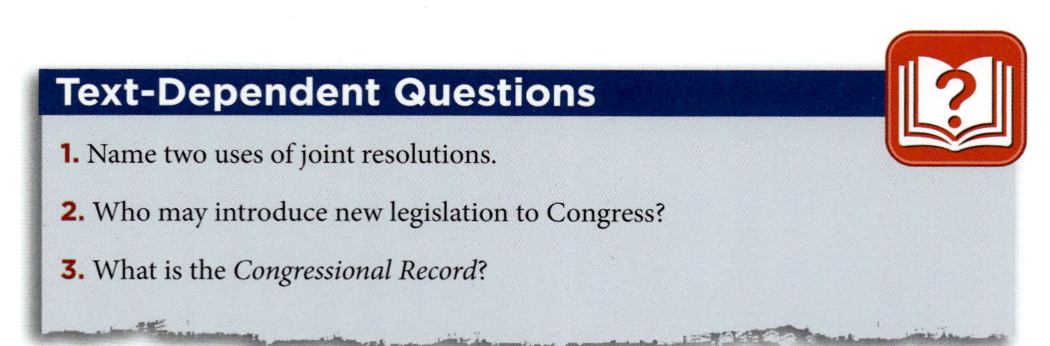

Text-Dependent Questions

1. Name two uses of joint resolutions.

2. Who may introduce new legislation to Congress?

3. What is the *Congressional Record*?

Research Project

Find a bill sponsored by your representative to the House. Research its legislative number (i.e., "H.R." number), the date it was introduced, a summary of its contents, and significant actions as it moved through the legislative process. Write a brief report summarizing your findings, including information about committees the bill was referred to and whether it was ultimately signed into law.

Consideration by Committee

Words to Understand

Annul: To declare something invalid.

Interrogation: The process of questioning someone to obtain information.

Subpoena: A formal document ordering someone to provide evidence or testimony, most often to a court.

Testimony: A formal statement, either spoken or in writing, provided to a court of law or legislative body.

Every bill introduced to Congress is assigned to a committee or subcommittee and added to its legislative calendar. The primary purpose of a congressional committee is to determine whether or not a bill would make a good law. Based on that determination, the committee presents a recommendation to the chamber of Congress into which the bill was originally introduced. Only those bills valued by the committee chairperson are considered, however. A bill that is not considered will not be addressed at all by the committee. The bill simply "dies" in committee and makes no further progress toward becoming a law.

For those bills that are considered by committee, this early phase in the lawmaking process is also the most critical. As a bill progresses through Congress, it is typically amended at every stage to provide clarity, address new concerns, or document a compromise, but never is a bill under more

Representative for California's 43rd District, Maxine Waters, and former senator Hillary Clinton.

scrutiny than during committee consideration. The assigned committee or subcommittee conducts an intensive study of each bill to understand its potential impact and determine the proposed law's necessity and feasibility of enforcement. Committees often hold public hearings to collect the facts required to make their recommendations and file committee reports.

Committee Hearings

Committees are usually made up of those members of Congress who have the most prior experience in the committee's field of interest. In some cases, the members of a committee themselves have the knowledge necessary to make an informed determination on a bill. If necessary, the committee may consult with federal agencies, such as the Government Accountability Office and the president's Office of Management and Budget, to ensure that a law, if passed, will be adequately funded and supported. Complex bills, however, require additional input from experts, government officials, and other associated individuals. In order to obtain this information, the committee calls a hearing.

Committee hearings are public proceedings, similar to court trials, during which witnesses provide **testimony** representing all sides of a legislative issue. Unless the topic under consideration is likely to reveal classified information or compromise national security, committee hearings are open to public observation. Audio transcripts are kept for future use by committee members and distributed to other interested members of Congress. The press often reports on hearings of national interest. In fact, members of the public who are interested in this aspect of the legislative process may watch televised hearings on the cable network C-SPAN, which regularly broadcasts House and Senate committee proceedings.

The committee selects the witnesses it would like to testify during the hearing. Generally, there are individuals who favor a bill and those who oppose it, and a committee hears from both sides. In addition, objective experts in the field may testify on a proposed law's impact regardless of their personal opinion. If a witness chooses not to participate, the committee has the authority to serve a **subpoena**, forcing the potential witness to testify or face jail time. Once again, the majority party has great influence because the committee often invites more witnesses who support the majority's position on the bill.

Hearings are often used as a forum for committee members to publicly present their views on an issue. Prior to witness testimony, the chairperson reads a statement

Above, a special Senate Subcommittee of the Committee on Commerce meets at the Waldorf-Astoria hotel to question individuals involved in the disastrous sinking of the ship Titanic. *Generally, congressional committees' primary role is to review legislation; however, when circumstances demand it, ad hoc committees can be convened for investigations.*

expressing his or her initial thoughts. The ranking member follows with a speech from the minority point of view. Witnesses must submit their testimony to the committee in writing before the hearing. During the proceedings, the witness reads a summary and then answers questions posed by committee members. Committee rules impose a time limit on witness testimony, with each committee member receiving equal **interrogation** time. Once all witnesses have testified, the hearing ends.

Committee hearings are important steps in the lawmaking process because they involve the participation of regular citizens in drafting legislation. By listening

to the testimonials of people who would be directly affected by a new law, committee members can take into consideration the public's concerns and modify the bill to create legislation that appeals to the majority of the American people. A bill that is recommended favorably by a committee is often vastly different from the draft that is first introduced to Congress. This is because of the inclusion of amendments to address concerns raised during hearings and those added during the markup phase.

Legislation Markup

Following the hearings, committee members assemble for a series of markup meetings. These meetings are meant to ensure that the committee completely understands the meaning of a bill and agrees with its purpose. Armed with the testimony presented during the hearings, committee members may modify, add, and delete components of the original bill to create a version that addresses their concerns and their constituents' needs. Like committee hearings, markup meetings are held in open sessions. The proceedings are not recorded or distributed, however, which encourages lawmakers to be more candid with their concerns and more creative in exploring compromises.

Markup meetings rarely begin with a review of the legislation as originally introduced to Congress. Instead, the committee chairperson usually takes the first swipe at modifying the bill and presents to the committee what is known as the *chairperson's mark*. This version is the chairperson's recommendation for approval. The amendments typically address the chairperson's own concerns as well as input from influential sources. These include majority party leadership and lobbyists with whom the chairperson may have discussed the legislation. Although the chairperson has a powerful role, other committee members debate the changes and offer further amendments during the markup meetings.

Committee members go over the bill very carefully, reading the document line by line and discussing each one in detail before moving on to the next. If a committee member has a concern with a line, he or she may propose an amendment, such as changing a line to eliminate a conflict, adding text to clarify a definition, or removing a line altogether. The committee votes on each proposed amendment and, if approved by a majority, adds the change to the document. Any proposed amendment must be germane to the subject, which means it is directly related to the line in question.

BYPASSING A COMMITTEE

A bill left to die in committee has one slight chance of proceeding to the full chamber for a vote. If the committee chairperson does not take action on an assigned bill for 30 or more legislative days, a member of Congress may present a motion to discharge the bill from committee. In this rarely used process, the motion remains open with the journal clerk, and members of Congress outside the committee may add their signatures in support. If a majority of the chamber into which the motion was introduced signs the document, it is entered into the *Congressional Record* and added to the Calendar of Motions to Discharge Committees.

After the measure to discharge the committee has been on the calendar for at least seven days, any signing member may call for recognition of the motion on the chamber floor. Members of the chamber debate the motion for a maximum of 20 minutes; equal time is spent arguing for and against the measure. Following the debate, a signing member may request that the chamber immediately consider the bill. If the chamber agrees to this motion, the full chamber considers the original bill under the standard legislative process, effectively bypassing committee consideration.

If the committee favorably reports a heavily marked bill, the multiple amendments may actually reduce the bill's chances for approval. During the full chamber vote, members of Congress consider each amendment individually and may reject the entire legislation because of a disagreement with a single amendment. As a solution, the committee chairperson may draft a new bill that combines the text of the original with committee changes. The chairperson introduces this "clean" bill to Congress following the standard procedure. When the clean bill, under a new legislative number, is reassigned to the committee, the committee immediately reports favorably with no changes.

The legislation markup phase is the stage in the lawmaking process where most legislation is written. Bills often receive additional amendments in subsequent stages of the process, but those changes, too, must be germane to the legislation and cannot alter the overarching meaning or directive of a bill reported by committee.

Senators Orrin Hatch and Arlen Specter during a hearing of the Senate Committee on the Judiciary in 2007.

The influence a senator or representative wields during this process is what makes a congressional committee or subcommittee seat such a highly desirable post. During chamber sessions, members may vote on measures and offer amendment proposals, but their greatest involvement in making new laws comes during committee markup sessions.

Committee Report

With the markup phase complete, the committee votes to determine whether to recommend the bill to the chamber of Congress into which it was introduced. A simple majority decides the fate of the bill, and committee votes are recorded to inform the public as to which way each member voted. Whether the committee reports on the

CONGRESSIONAL RECOMMENDATIONS

Committees may make one of a variety of recommendations on the bill to Congress:

Report favorably without amendment: Recommends passage of the original bill or a clean bill.

Report favorably with amendment: Recommends passage of the original bill with changes.

Report unfavorably: Recommends rejection of the bill.

Table the bill: When a committee tables a bill, it takes no further action and the bill "dies" in committee. Committees rarely report a bill unfavorably; instead, they table it—essentially rejecting the bill before it comes to a vote in the chamber.

bill as introduced to Congress, on a marked-up version, or on a clean bill, the time spent in the hearing and markup phases is invaluable. A written report accompanying the committee's recommendation provides expert guidance on the proposed law and its anticipated impact on U.S. citizens.

Together with its recommendation, the committee distributes to Congress a detailed report of the bill. This report contains all the information accumulated by the committee (including transcripts of hearing proceedings and meeting notes) during its consideration and is a valuable resource for members of Congress as they prepare to vote on the bill in their respective chambers. A typical report begins with a description of the bill, the purpose of the proposed legislation, and the reasons behind the committee's recommendation. If the committee recommends a bill with amendments, each amendment is explained, and the reason for its inclusion is justified.

The report also provides comprehensive information on the projected impact of the bill if passed into law. Any existing laws affected, particularly those that would be **annulled**, or made inoperable, by the proposed legislation, must be listed. In addition, the estimated annual costs of enforcement, projected five years into the future, must be included. Finally, the voting record of the bill is attached; this

The legislative calendar provides crucial dates for the legislative process.

indicates how committee members voted on each amendment as well as on the final draft. In closing, committee members may add additional statements to the report. Those members who voted in the minority often take this opportunity to express their reasons for dissent.

A bill reported by committee is added to the legislative calendar of the appropriate chamber of Congress. To have adequate time to study the document before taking a final vote, members of Congress must have access to the report at least three weekdays during which Congress is in session. The committee chairperson coordinates the prompt delivery of the completed report to the Government Printing Office for distribution to all members of Congress. Today, committee reports are also made available in a digital version for faster turnaround and e-mail delivery to senators and representatives who are traveling on business.

It is impossible to overstate the importance of committee consideration in passing a law, but its value truly extends beyond the legislative process. If a proposed bill becomes law, the information collected by the committee or subcommittee is included as part of its legislative history and is often revisited to serve additional purposes. For example, a committee report may be used in the judicial process as an excellent resource for interpreting the intention of the law. The work that senators and representatives accomplish as members of committees is only one aspect of their roles. Equally important is time spent participating in legislative action on the Senate and House floors.

Text-Dependent Questions

1. What is the primary purpose of a congressional committee?
2. Are congressional committee hearings open to the public?
3. What is meant by a "clean" bill?

Research Project

Either on television or through the official Web site (C-SPAN.org), watch footage of Congress in action. Take notes as you watch, recording who is speaking, what they are speaking about, any textual commentary provided, and other features. Write a brief report giving an overview of the coverage. Bonus: Research information about any legislation you saw being discussed, and include this as a supplement to your report.

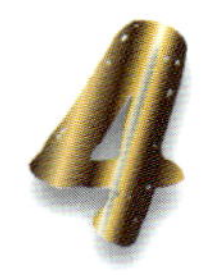

Initial House Action

Words to Understand

Pending: Still awaiting finalization.

Quorum: The minimum number of participants of a group required to conduct business.

Unanimous: When a group is in total agreement on something.

A bill introduced to Congress is assigned to a committee, which considers it and then reports on it back to Congress, either favorably or adversely. If the bill is introduced in the House of Representatives, this entire process takes place in the House; if it originates in the Senate, the same process occurs in the Senate. The next three chapters of this book follow the bill as it gains approval from each chamber of Congress. Although the process is very similar in both chambers, here we will describe a bill introduced to the House, the most common path for a new law.

The House of Representatives considers a bill reported by a committee in very much the same way the committee or subcommittee addresses a bill. The main difference is the amount of time spent with the legislation. Representatives do not have adequate time to thoroughly study and debate every bill, which is why the committee report is so valuable and why noncommittee members must have the report in hand so they can read it at least three days prior to House consideration. During initial House

Nancy Pelosi was the first woman Speaker and the highest-ranking woman elected official in U.S. history.

action, the bill will be added to a legislative calendar, prioritized for consideration, presented, debated, and voted on by the chamber.

Order of Business

Committees specialize in specific areas of legislation; therefore, consideration of a new bill does not vary widely from one bill to the next, and the process is fairly simple. On the House floor, however, the process is more complex because the chamber must be prepared for any type of bill—public or private, taxing or appropriation, and all others. As a result, the House employs multiple legislative calendars and other rules to prioritize and nominate bills for consideration. This strict order of business may sound confusing, but it is essential to maintaining an effective legislative process in the House.

When a bill is reported to the House of Representatives, the Speaker of the House assigns it to one of three legislative calendars: the Calendar of the Committee of the Whole House on the State of the Union (or simply the Union Calendar), the House Calendar, or the Private Calendar. The Union Calendar is used to schedule public bills for raising revenue, apportioning funds, or authorizing payments. The House Calendar receives any public bills not covered by the Union Calendar, and the Private Calendar posts all private bills. The majority of new legislation is typically assigned to the Union Calendar.

The process to get a bill off a calendar and onto the House floor for debating is referred to as the *call of committees*. Every Wednesday, the Speaker of the House calls on each standing committee in order. When a committee is called, that committee's chairperson may request that the House consider any bill reported favorably by the committee that has been posted to a House calendar for at least one day. If the Speaker cannot get through all committees in a single session, the call resumes the following day. A committee may not be called on again until all other committees are called in the current round.

The House consideration process maintains the flow of legislation through the chamber. Although committee chairpersons have the authority to prioritize the order in which their bills are considered, their authority does not extend to the House's overall agenda. In order for a high-priority bill to reach the House floor out of order, the chairperson of the committee reporting the bill must request a resolution from the Committee on Rules calling for immediate or subsequent consideration of the bill in question. In extreme cases—known as *closed rules*—the resolution may allow a bill to bypass the House floor amendment phase.

Paul Ryan served as the 54th Speaker of the United States House of Representatives from October 2015 to January 2019.

Even with multiple legislative calendars and rules in place, the order of business may be altered by **unanimous** consent. On rare occasions, the Speaker of the House and the minority leader agree on a bill's importance and assign it privileged status. Bills that address national security or public health issues often fall into this category. The committee chairperson responsible for reporting a bill with privileged status may call that legislation for immediate consideration anytime during session when no other business is **pending**. Privileged or not, once called from the calendar, consideration of a bill begins immediately on the House floor.

House Floor

Any member of the House may participate in consideration of a bill on the House floor. The Speaker of the House moderates the process, and all participating representatives address only the Speaker. One majority and one minority member of the committee that reported the bill represent their respective sides as floor managers during debate. These speakers typically give a speech about the bill and then share the remainder of their allocated debate time with other interested representatives, often the author and sponsors of the bill. The consideration process differs between bills assigned to the House Calendar and those assigned to the Union Calendar.

Bills assigned to the House Calendar are not eligible for amendment. The consideration process is simple, and debate time is relatively short: After the House clerk reads the bill, speakers are granted 40 minutes, equally divided between each side of the issue, to debate the proposed legislation. Speakers use this time to present information supporting their positions on the bill in attempt to influence other representatives to vote their way. Because of the limited time for debate, some members might not have an opportunity to speak but may present a written document to ensure their positions appear in the *Congressional Record.*

Bills on the Union Calendar follow a more complex procedure, which allows for in-depth debate and amendments. To accommodate this process, the House of Representatives functions like a standing committee, called the Committee of the Whole House on the State of the Union (the Committee of the Whole). As part of this transformation, the Speaker of the House appoints a committee chairperson to run the debate, then steps down. When the Committee of the Whole completes consideration of a bill, the chamber either considers another bill from the Union Calendar or transitions back to the House of Representatives.

Consideration by the Committee of the Whole begins with the first reading of the bill. The procedure follows that of regular House debates, but each side is allowed one full hour to address the committee. Following debate, the clerk reads the bill a second time, launching the amendment phase. Like a standing committee, the Committee of the Whole reviews the bill section by section, and members may propose amendments. Only amendments that receive majority approval are accepted. Anytime during this phase, a member may move to end the process. If the committee passes the motion, the bill, with all approved amendments, is read a final time.

Because of time restrictions and the high number of members seeking to participate in House action, the pace of the floor debate and consideration by

Members of the U.S. House of Representatives walk the floor of the House chamber as they are called to vote on a resolution. After a clerk gives the final reading of the bill under consideration, the Speaker of the House immediately calls for a vote.

the Committee of the Whole is incredibly fast. The Speaker's role as moderator is essential to maintaining order, which enables the House of Representatives to pack as much business as possible into a legislative day. The Speaker is responsible for managing the clock, approving each member who addresses the chamber, and more. Following the clerk's final reading of a bill under consideration, the Speaker immediately calls a House vote.

Voting Process

A bill matures as it travels through the House of Representatives from introduction to vote—its content evolves with the addition of amendments that broaden the legislation's appeal. Along the way, the number of representatives backing the bill grows. Introduced by a single member of Congress, the bill likely will have picked up cosponsors before becoming the focus of a committee. It leaves the committee with

QUORUM

A **quorum** is the minimum number of participants required to conduct business. Its purpose is to encourage attendance because it enables activity to continue in a member's absence. In the U.S. Congress, a quorum is a simple majority (218 representatives or 51 senators). If the number of members present for a vote appears to be less than a quorum, the Speaker orders a quorum call, which takes the form of a roll call, conducted by the House clerk, or a recorded call using the electronic voting devices. Following the call, a present member may move to force absent members to appear in the chamber.

When the House is acting as the Committee of the Whole, only 100 representatives are needed to form a quorum. This happens because debate goes into further detail on fewer bills, so fewer members participate on each bill. If a quorum is not present, the chairperson orders a quorum call during the amendment phase, because the committee must vote on proposed amendments. In order to speed the process, the call ends as soon as it reaches 100 members. If a quorum is not reached, however, the committee rises and resolves to the House of Representatives, enabling the legislative day to continue.

the backing of a political party and is finally considered by an entire chamber that is well versed in the bill's contents through the committee report. A vote determines whether the bill has support from the majority of the House.

The call for a House vote is a routine action. The Speaker asks, "As many as are in favor of [name of the bill], say, 'Aye.' As many as are opposed, say, 'No.'" All members of the House of Representatives present in the chamber may vote on the bill. Bills assigned to the House Calendar require a three-fifths majority in order to pass. For example, if 100 people vote, 60 of them must be in favor to approve a

bill. A bill called from the Union Calendar, however, needs only a simple majority (i.e., 51 out of 100) to be approved.

The Speaker determines the result by the response volume. If he or she hears more "Ayes" than "Nos," the Speaker declares the bill passed. When a vote is too close to call, the Speaker may order a division vote, in which representatives stand up rather than call out to cast their votes. The Speaker counts standing members to calculate the vote. The final option is an electronic vote. Representatives cast their votes using an electronic voting station, which counts automatically and accurately. This method is foolproof, but because there are a limited number of voting stations, it is time consuming, so it is rarely used.

Bills that make it to a vote are important to the parties that supported them through the legislative process. If that party is the voting minority, it has an opportunity

Above is an 1890 photograph of the House of Representatives chamber, taken from the balcony while the House was in session. Today, many House votes are taken as they would have been in 1890, with the passage of a bill determined by the response volume of "Ayes" versus "Nos."

to keep the bill alive. The bill's floor manager may call a motion to reconsider the bill and try to win a future vote. The Speaker typically grants this request without debate and reassigns the bill to committee. A representative interested in adding a final amendment may motion to recommit with instructions. This motion is debatable, as both parties wish to influence what instructions appear when the bill is reconsidered.

Representatives are the voices of the people in Congress, and they are elected for two basic reasons: to draft legislation that benefits the constituents of their congressional districts and all United States citizens, and to represent constituents' interests when voting on other new laws under consideration. Politics are built on the foundation of compromise, however, and in order for representatives to get things done, at times they must give other members of Congress what they need—votes. Fortunately, legislators have a couple of tricks they can use to help a fellow member without voting against the interests of their own constituents.

In a "catch-and-release" deal—to "catch" the number required for a majority—a party leader persuades minority representatives to promise their votes. Although

Since the Sandy Hook Massacre in 2012, Senator Chris Murphy has taken a strong stance on gun reform. Since the shooting, he has participated in several debates on the House floor. In 2016, the Senate failed to pass four separate gun control amendments to a Department of Justice spending bill.

their constituents might disapprove, these representatives may agree, in exchange for guaranteed future votes from the majority party. If the leader secures more votes than required, however, the representative is "released" from the deal. Then, the bill passes, and the member votes as his constituents expect. "Pairing" is another method. A representative who is persuaded to vote against his constituents' desires pairs up with a member on the opposite side. Both vote "Present" rather than in favor or opposition; these votes do not change the outcome, but the representative does not record a vote that is unpopular with his constituents.

Text-Dependent Questions

1. Name the three legislative calendars in the House of Representatives.
2. Who may participate in consideration of a bill on the House floor?
3. What majority is required for bills assigned to the House Calendar in order to pass?

Research Project

Go to the home page of the *Congressional Record* (https://www.congress.gov/congressional-record). Select a day from the previous week, and examine the activities of both chambers of Congress. Take notes on what you read, including bills and resolutions introduced, reports filed, and committee or joint meetings held. Create a visual diagram that organizes all of this information and shows how the congressional day was spent.

Senate Review

Words to Understand

Engrossed: In legal terms, the presentation of a document in its final form.

Filibuster: To speak at length in order to delay a vote in a legislative assembly.

Waive: To refrain from enforcing a rule, restriction, or other claim.

A bill introduced to, and passed by, the House of Representatives is referred to the Senate for consideration. It is important to remember that the House and Senate are equal partners in passing legislation. The Senate does not review House bills as a superior body of Congress; it reviews them from a different perspective. Whereas House members represent proportional numbers of constituents, senators represent states equally. By the same token, the House reviews all bills introduced and passed in the Senate. Similar to initial House action, review by the Senate involves committee consideration, floor debates and amendments to the bill, and chamber votes.

In general, the Senate consideration process is very similar to the House process, as both are based on Thomas Jefferson's *Manual of Parliamentary Practice*. The House reasserts its procedural rules at the start of each new Congress. By contrast, the Senate functions largely by the rules established during the first Congress in 1789, and the manner in which business is conducted is quite different from the House. Pace of activity is another key difference. Because there are fewer members generating legislation, more committee assignments per senator, and longer debate times, the Senate pace is much slower than that of the House.

Senator Orrin Hatch has been the president pro tempore since 2015.

Referral to Senate

When a bill passes a body of Congress, it formally becomes an act. Immediately upon approval, the House sends a written message to the Senate chamber indicating the change of status, and the Senate prepares to receive an **engrossed** copy of the act for review. The engrossed copy is a final version of the legislation prepared by the House enrolling clerk. It is crucial that the engrossed copy contain the text of the bill exactly as approved by the House, because both bodies of Congress must pass completely identical versions in order to advance the legislation to the next step.

To draft an engrossed copy of a bill, the enrollment clerk combines the version reported by the standing committee with the amendments approved during initial House action. The enrollment clerk pays special attention to the order in which the amendments were introduced and the precise wording and punctuation agreed to by House members. This process can be quite challenging, particularly with a heavily amended bill. Today, some bills receive more than 100 amendments, pushing the average length of a bill to more than 19 pages. An engrossed act received by the secretary of the Senate is ready for committee assignment.

The Senate has fewer standing committees than the House, but the committee consideration process is the same in each chamber. Sometimes, however, identical bills are introduced in both places at the same time, to increase the chances of passing. These are called *companion bills*. If the companion bill is approved by the House and assigned to a Senate committee, the committee indefinitely postpones the Senate version and considers only the approved House act. If the Senate is considering a similar bill when the House bill passes, the Senate committee may add elements of its bill to the House act in the form of amendments.

At the close of the committee consideration phase, the assigned Senate committee prepares a report and presents the legislation to the Senate floor. As described in Chapter 3, the act may be reported favorably or adversely, clean or with amendments. During the opening proceedings of each new legislative day, the presiding officer calls for the filing of committee reports. At this time, the committee representative may speak to the chamber about the act and communicate his or her position. However, this opportunity is rarely taken, and senators typically hand the report to a chamber clerk in document form.

Legislative days are different from calendar days: a legislative day is a period of conducting business. A new legislative day begins when the previous one adjourns, as indicated by the presiding officer, who declares an official order to indicate the close

Senator Robert Byrd of Tennessee set a new record when he won his ninth Senate term. Byrd became the president pro tempore of the Senate in January 2007 and was the Senate majority leader for two separate terms during his tenure.

of business. In the morning, the Senate continues its work. When business is complete, the presiding officer adjourns the legislative day. Legislative days may last several calendar days or even weeks.

Senate Chamber

Although the legislative procedure of the Senate is similar to that of the House, the manner in which the Senate conducts business is substantially different. In the House, strict adherence to the rules is necessary to manage a large chamber with 435 members generating thousands of bills every session. In the Senate, with 100 senators serving six-year terms, the order of business can be more flexible. Senators actually have more influence over the flow of legislation than the presiding officer, which is in stark contrast to the House of Representatives, where the Speaker tightly controls the order of business.

The Senate maintains one calendar to track legislation, the Calendar of Business, on which all introduced bills and approved acts appear, regardless of type. Each legislative day, as part of morning business, the presiding officer conducts the call of the calendar, which is a process to address pending business. When the next reported act comes up, if there are no objections, the chamber may begin consideration. This rule, however, is rarely used. Senators usually prefer to **waive** the calendar call in favor of addressing legislation in order of priority or efficiency.

To address an act outside the order prescribed by the Calendar of Business, a senator presents a motion to the presiding officer to consider the legislation. A motion is commonly used to consider an uncomplicated act immediately after its report, and requires unanimous consent from the Senate chamber. If granted, the presiding officer allocates time for debate, and floor consideration begins. If another senator objects to the motion, the act remains on the Calendar of Business and may be taken up during a future call. If the Senate requires no debate or amendments, a quick vote removes the act from the calendar.

Motions to consider legislation out of order are typically made by the Senate majority leader. Although the Senate does not adhere to its legislative calendar as

Senator Chuck Schumer represents New York and is the minority leader as of 2018.

SYSTEM OF LIGHTS AND BELLS

Senators and representatives are busier than ever before. The average hours spent working per week, days per year, and bills introduced per Congress have increased greatly over time. Because of the heavy workload and the fact that sessions may operate with only a quorum present, senators and representatives appear in their respective chambers only when required to do so. More often, they can be found working in their offices or other parts of the Capitol Building, so Congress utilizes a system of lights and bells that signal throughout these areas to inform members of Congress of important developments in the chambers.

The tools of the system are simple enough (consisting of a bell and two lights, side by side). The system itself is complex, however, because of the many combinations of rings and lights necessary to communicate the various messages, particularly in the House, which includes specific codes for the Committee of the Whole. Utilizing this system, messages can be communicated to absent legislators regarding quorum calls, votes, adjournment, recess, and more. When a recorded vote is called, the alert is sent after the first member registers a vote. Remaining members have 15 minutes in which to appear in the chamber and record their votes.

strictly as the House of Representatives, there is an order of business, which is unofficially controlled by the majority leader. The majority leader meets regularly with members of his or her party and the minority leader to identify Senate priorities and agree on which acts to consider next. This type of process works well in the Senate, where agendas, as well as the deals brokered around each new piece of legislation, change on a daily basis.

When a motion to consider an act receives unanimous consent, it is usually not a surprise—in fact, very few legislative bombshells get dropped on the Senate floor, thanks to the work of the Republican Legislative Scheduling Office and the Democratic Policy Committee. These service groups partner with their respective party members and leaders to facilitate communication regarding legislative issues, priorities, and procedural plans. They provide the information that party leaders need to devise their floor strategies, down to predicted senator responses to motions.

Political party alignment becomes even more important when the Senate chamber considers an act for approval.

Floor Consideration

Once an act is recognized for consideration, one senator from each party represents his or her side of the issue as floor manager throughout the debate. These senators are typically the chairperson and ranking member of the committee that holds jurisdiction over the act. Floor managers speak first and then yield the floor to other senators, usually members of the same party, who present prepared statements in support of their positions on the act. Senate rules impose no limits on the number

Senate Majority Leader Mitch McConnell sits down with President Obama.

of senators who may speak or the length of their speeches. This is a significant and noticeable difference between the two chambers of Congress.

The primary goal of speaking during floor debate is to win the votes of any undecided senators. Presentations often include facts and charts, based on research data collected during committee hearings, to illustrate important points. Senate debate is a public event, which is broadcast live on the cable television channel C-SPAN2. The proceedings are recorded and printed in the *Congressional Record*, which is also available to read online at the Library of Congress Web site. Although senators may address only the presiding officer during debate, they use this opportunity to sway public opinion as well as that of their colleagues.

Sometimes, the goal of speaking during debate is to delay the vote. Senators on the minority side typically state their cases and graciously accept defeat, but occasionally, when they are ardently opposed to an act, they use the only tool available to halt the process—the **filibuster**. Because Senate rules do not limit speech length, senators may delay a vote by simply speaking at great length. In 1957, South Carolina Senator Strom Thurmond spoke nonstop for over 24 hours in opposition to a proposed law. This tactic is most effective with a united political party, but even a single senator can make an impact.

Eventually, both sides in the debate complete their arguments for and against the act, and the floor managers yield their time back to the presiding officer. The presiding officer then requests the final reading of the act and calls for a vote. The Senate usually employs the roll call voting method, in which the legislative clerk reads each senator's name in alphabetical order, and the senator responds, "Aye" in favor of the legislation or "No" in opposition. The Senate requires a simple majority to pass an act, and, as in the House of Representatives, a quorum is necessary to vote.

The presiding officer votes only to break a tie. When all votes are calculated and a result determined, the presiding officer announces the act's passage or defeat. Following the announcement, the party leader for the losing side typically requests a motion to reconsider the act. This motion is a mere formality, though, as the majority side simply tables it, thus marking the vote as the final Senate action for the legislation in its present form. If the Senate passed the act, the next step in its journey toward becoming law depends on whether or not the Senate amended the legislation.

A proposed law must pass both the House of Representatives and the Senate in identical form to receive congressional approval. If the Senate passed the act without amendment, then the legislation is approved for submission to the White House and presidential action. If the Senate edited or modified the act in any way, however, the legislation returns to the House for final review and vote on the amended version. Most new laws require a return to the chamber of introduction. This book assumes a Senate-modified act, so our legislation, along with Senate amendments, returns to the House of Representatives.

Vice President Mike Pence and members of Congress celebrate the passing of a new tax bill on the White House's South Lawn in 2018.

Text-Dependent Questions

1. Who authored the *Manual of Parliamentary Practice* used by the House and Senate?
2. How is an engrossed copy of a bill prepared?
3. What is the name of the calendar the Senate maintains to track legislation?

Research Project

Research a recent (within the past ten years) use of the filibuster in Congress. Write a brief report including details on who issued the filibuster, the act being debated, the person's reasons for filibustering, and the political results. Bonus: Include information on the filibusterer's biography and how the news media analyzed the importance of the filibuster.

Final Congressional Approval

Words to Understand

Conference Committee: In the U.S. Congress, a temporary committee made up of both House and Senate members, organized to prepare a version of an act that incorporates amendments from both chambers.

Dissenting: Expressing disagreement with a majority.

Page: A student who assists with the functioning of Congress, including preparing the chambers for each day's legislative session and providing general assistance to legislators and chamber staff.

A bill introduced into the House of Representatives and passed by the House is then submitted to the Senate for consideration. The Senate often changes the House-approved act based on new information discovered during committee hearings, fresh perspectives argued in debate, or related ideas in pending legislation, and votes on an edited version. These changes, known as *amendments*, may take the form of a word or section added to the act, removed, or edited to alter its meaning. Ideally, through effective negotiation and amendments, legislators will broaden an act's appeal until majorities in both chambers support its passage.

The Senate side of the U.S. Capitol Building in Washington, D.C.

HIGH SCHOOL STUDENTS IN THE SENATE

Working as a Senate **page** provides the ultimate perspective for young people interested in observing our government's lawmaking process. Pages are responsible for preparing the chamber for each day's session and providing general assistance to legislators and chamber staff. Pages are most often seen running documents around the Capitol complex. Their presence enables lawmakers to focus on the business at hand, transitioning from one bill to the next without a lapse in productivity. There was a House page program, but it was suspended in 2011.

All Senate pages must be at least high school juniors during their time of service, which may include summer sessions before or after their junior years. In addition to working in the Senate, pages enjoy preferred access to Washington, D.C., area museums, and other points of interest. To become a page, a student must be sponsored by a senator from his or her state of residence. Additional requirements include maintaining a 3.0 GPA, providing letters of recommendation, writing essays, and participating in an interview process. If you wish to be a page, contact your state senators to request a nomination.

not always the House of Representatives). During initial review in the Senate, the committee chairperson may recognize that because of extensive amendments, the Senate version is not likely to pass the House as is. In that case, the Senate majority leader, on submitting the engrossed bill to the House, may motion to call a conference committee, thus placing negotiation in the hands of the conference committee and disabling the House chairperson's option to amend Senate amendments.

Conference Committee

Often referred to as the "Third House of Congress," a conference committee is itself a powerful legislative body focused on advancing acts deadlocked between the Senate and the House of Representatives. After the second chamber agrees to the requesting chamber's motion for a conference committee, the Speaker of the House and Senate presiding officer select committee members to address the act under consideration.

The conference may convene a single time or conduct a series of meetings. Once the conference comes to a compromise, it submits its recommendation in the form of a report to both chambers of Congress, and the committee is dissolved.

Although the conference committee meets as one entity, it is actually made up of two subgroups representing the House and the Senate. Each body assigns a number of its members (usually, 7–11). Conference committee members are called *managers* or, more informally, *conferees*. The number of conferees in a subgroup is not significant, because when called upon to make a decision on an amendment, the groups each vote with a single voice. Conference committee members must work within their group to come to a majority decision, which is then communicated as that congressional body's united position on the issue.

Because of the importance of conference committee decisions, the majority party leaders in each body (the Speaker of the House and the Senate presiding officer) handpick the conferees. Senior members of the committees that considered the act under its initial review in the House and the Senate, such as the committee chairpersons and ranking members, are typically appointed, and chairpersons may be advised by other chamber members on additional members. When an act is of particular interest to the majority party, though, the party leaders are sure to assign legislators whom they expect will promote an outcome that is most beneficial to majority party interests.

The conference committee receives the engrossed act and any further amendments. Seeking to eliminate disputes, the committee considers only controversial amendments. It may not alter sections agreed to by both chambers. Any compromise the committee suggests must be germane to the act, meaning it must not introduce new information. If an issue under dispute is a number (for example, if an amendment were to change a "5" to a "10"), the committee must agree on a figure between 5 and 10. If an issue is in the text, the amendment must be rewritten to the approval of the conference without adding content nonexistent elsewhere in the document.

After the conference committee considers the engrossed act, it reports to Congress its recommendation for advancement of the legislation. The conference addresses each disputed amendment based on the following four options:

1. The Senate recedes from all (or certain of) its amendments.
2. The House recedes from its disagreement with all (or certain of) the Senate amendments and agree thereto.

Conference committee members are chosen from the House and Senate to represent each body's concerns.

3. The House recedes from its disagreement with all (or certain of) the Senate amendments and agree thereto with amendments.
4. The House recedes from all (or certain of) its amendments to the Senate amendments or its amendments to the Senate bill.

If the conference committee cannot agree on some amendments, the report must include a statement explaining the conflicting recommendations. If, after a period of 20 calendar days and 10 legislative days, the conference reaches no agreement at all, replacement conferees are appointed to keep the negotiations moving forward. Once complete, a majority of each conference group signs the report, which is printed and distributed to each chamber of Congress. The final report is a detailed document that describes conference committee recommendations and their impact on the legislation. This document is the basis for final congressional consideration of the act.

Final Consideration

A conference committee report contains joint recommendations from the two bodies of Congress for reconciling amendments to an act that were not initially agreed to by both chambers. If both bodies agree to the recommendations, then the act takes the next step toward becoming law. The chambers consider the report individually, beginning with the body that *accepted* the conference committee request. In the House, the report must be printed in the *Congressional Record* three calendar days prior to consideration to allow adequate preparation and debate. The Senate, which does not debate conference reports prior to consideration, may address the report immediately.

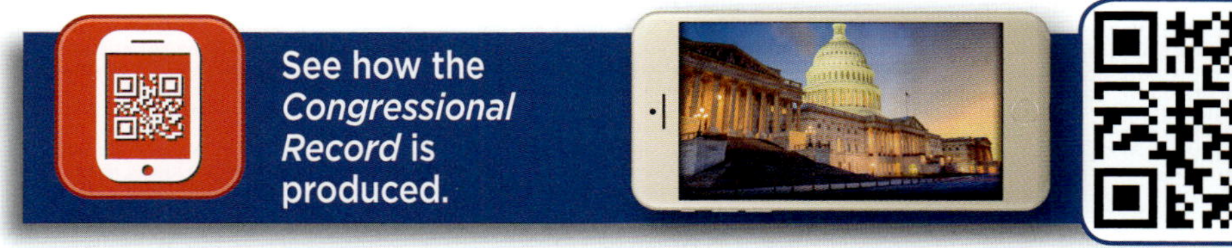

Conference report consideration is a high priority in both houses. Once available for consideration in the House or the Senate, the presiding officer typically addresses the report as the next order of business. Debate in the House is limited to one hour, equally divided between the majority and minority parties. If the House floor managers for each party agree in their support of the report, then any opposing members may represent the **dissenting** position for one-third of the allotted debate time. A conference report may not be amended during consideration; following debate, the chamber votes on adoption of the report as is.

If the first chamber to act on the conference report votes to reject its recommendations, then the report returns to the conference committee for further negotiation. If the chamber accepts the report, however, the official papers are

United States
of America

Congressional Record

PROCEEDINGS AND DEBATES OF THE 106th CONGRESS, FIRST SESSION

Vol. 145 WASHINGTON, FRIDAY, FEBRUARY 12, 1999 *No. 26*

Senate

The Senate met at 9:36 a.m. and was called to order by the Chief Justice of the United States.

TRIAL OF WILLIAM JEFFERSON CLINTON, PRESIDENT OF THE UNITED STATES

The CHIEF JUSTICE. The Senate will convene as a Court of Impeachment. The Chaplain will offer a prayer.

PRAYER

The Chaplain, Dr. Lloyd John Ogilvie, offered the following prayer:

Gracious God, whose love for this Nation has been displayed so magnificently through our history, we praise You that Your presence fills this historic Chamber and enters into the minds of the Senators gathered here. Each of them is here by Your divine appointment. Together they claim Your promise, "Call upon Me in the day of trouble: I will deliver you."—Ps.50:15. We call upon You on this day of trouble in America as this impeachment trial comes to a close. You have enabled an honest, open debate of alternative solutions. Soon a vote will be taken. You have established a spirit of unity in the midst of differences. Most important of all, we know that we can trust You with the results. You can use what is decided and continue to accomplish Your plans for America. We entrust to Your care the President and his family. Use whatever is decided today to enable a deeper experience of Your grace in his life and healing in his family. We commit this day to You and thank You for the hope that fills our hearts as we place our complete trust in You. You are our Lord and Saviour. Amen.

The CHIEF JUSTICE. The Sergeant at Arms will make the proclamation.

The Sergeant at Arms, James W. Ziglar, made proclamation as follows:

Hear ye! Hear ye! Hear ye! All persons are commanded to keep silent, on pain of imprisonment, while the Senate of the United States is sitting for the trial of the articles of impeachment exhibited by the House of Representatives against William Jefferson Clinton, President of the United States.

THE JOURNAL

The CHIEF JUSTICE. If there is no objection, the Journal of proceedings of the trial are approved to date.

The majority leader is recognized.

Mr. LOTT. Thank you, Mr. Chief Justice.

ORDER OF PROCEDURE

Mr. LOTT. For the information of all Senators, later on today, the Secretary of the Senate will be putting at each Senator's desk something I think you will enjoy reading later. It is the prayers of the Chaplain during the impeachment trial. Subsequently, we plan to put it in a small pamphlet, because they truly have been magnificent. We thought you each would like to have copies.

The Senate will resume final deliberations now in the closed session. Thank goodness. At this point in the proceedings, there are approximately eight Members who still wish to speak or submit part of their speech into the RECORD.

Following those final speeches, the Senate will resume open session and proceed to the votes on the two articles of impeachment. I estimate that those votes will begin at approximately 11, 11:30. However, the exact time will depend on the length of the remaining speeches, and also we will have to have a few minutes to open the Chamber and the galleries so that our constituents and our families can enter the galleries if they would like to.

Following those votes, all Senators should remain at their desks as the Senate proceeds to several housekeeping items relating to the adjournment of the Court of Impeachment. So again, I emphasize, please, after the votes, don't rush out of the Chamber because we have some very important proceedings to attend to, and I think you will enjoy them if you will stay and participate.

Under the consent agreement reached last night, following those votes, a motion relating to censure may be offered by the Senator from California, Senator FEINSTEIN. If offered, Senator GRAMM will be recognized to offer a motion relative to the Feinstein motion, with a vote to occur on the Gramm motion. Therefore, Senators may anticipate an additional vote or votes following the votes on the articles.

I thank the Senators. And I believe we are ready to proceed to the closed session.

Mrs. BOXER. Will the majority leader yield for a question?

Mr. LOTT. Yes.

Mrs. BOXER. Will there be intervening debate or no debate on any of those votes?

Mr. LOTT. In the UC that was reached last night, I believe we have 2 hours, which will be equally divided, for Senators to submit statements at that point or to make speeches if they would like. So I presume—after the votes, yes.

Mrs. BOXER. That is the question. Yes.

Mr. LOTT. I presume we will go on for a couple hours—2 or 3 o'clock in the afternoon, yes.

UNANIMOUS-CONSENT AGREEMENT—PRINTING OF STATEMENTS IN THE RECORD AND PRINTING OF SENATE DOCUMENT OF IMPEACHMENT PROCEEDINGS

Mr. LOTT. I would like to clarify one other matter. Senators will recall the motion approved February 9, 1999, which permitted each Senator to place in the CONGRESSIONAL RECORD his or her own statements made during final deliberations in closed session.

I ask unanimous consent that public statements made by Senators subsequent to the approval of that motion, with respect to his or her own statements made during the closed session, be deemed to be in compliance with the Senate rules. This would permit a Senator to release to the public his or her

• This "bullet" symbol identifies statements or insertions which are not spoken by a Member of the Senate on the floor.

S1457

Printed on recycled paper.

Pictured here is a page from a 1999 edition of the Congressional Record *that was published during the impeachment trial of President Clinton.*

submitted to the second body for consideration. Following approval, the first chamber's group of conferees officially disbands, having fulfilled its duty. If the second chamber votes to accept the report, then the act has passed Congress and is prepared for presidential action. Because the first chamber disbanded its conferees, if rejected by the second chamber, the act cannot be recommitted to conference, so a motion must be made for a new conference committee to consider the act.

If a report under consideration includes conflicting recommendations, then after voting on the report, the chambers must vote on each disputed amendment. If the voting body submitted an amendment in question, that chamber may withdraw

Conferees prepare for the Senate-House Conference Committee meeting on the Tax Cuts and Jobs Act in December 2017.

the amendment to resolve the issue. If the other body submitted the amendment, the voting body may accept or amend the amendment and hope the other body accepts the change. If the chambers still cannot agree, the entire conference committee process begins again. It is possible that the congressional session will end while an act is under consideration. If that happens, then the legislation dies and must be reintroduced in the next session, if at all.

In the most typical scenario, both chambers of Congress accept the conference committee report, thus passing the act in identical form in each house. With this milestone met, all original papers generated during the legislative process are delivered to the originating chamber of Congress and submitted to the enrolling clerk. He or she prepares a clean version of the approved act in its final form and submits the document to the Government Printing Office, which prepares on parchment the official legislation for presidential action. At the close of the congressional session, all original papers are filed in the National Archives.

When you consider the various negotiating tools available to lawmakers during the final approval stage, you begin to understand the intricacies of the legislative process. This complexity ensures that any legislation reaching the president's desk has been very carefully considered from multiple perspectives—should it become law, it will be as fair as possible to the American people. On the other hand, the entire process can be simple, particularly when the same majority party with shared priorities leads both chambers. It is important to note that Congress presents legislation for presidential action as a *recommendation*. The president, too, plays a powerful role in passing new laws.

Text-Dependent Questions

1. What is the purpose of a conference committee?
2. Who selects the conferees of a conference committee?
3. What happens if a congressional session ends while an act is under consideration?

Research Project

Research information about the National Archives, including its purpose, what it stores, what archivists do, and the types of documents it keeps on file. Use the database on the official National Archives Web site (http://www.archives.gov) to research three different documents from different periods in history. Write a brief report of your experience, what you discovered, and what you learned about the history of the archives.

Presidential Action

Words to Understand

Line-item veto: The power of a chief executive to reject certain parts of a bill.

Pocket veto: When a president indirectly vetoes a bill by leaving it unsigned as a legislative session expires.

Slip law: A document containing the complete text of a new law along with its legislative history; often the law's first published form.

Presidential action takes place at the end of the process by which a bill is signed into law, but the president's influence can be felt all along the way. At the beginning of each calendar year, the president stands before both chambers of Congress as a whole to deliver the State of the Union Address. The address usually includes a look back at America's progress over the previous 12 months and a look forward, outlining presidential expectations from Congress in the coming year. During this speech, the president asks Congress to introduce and pass what he envisions as the legislation of greatest importance to the nation.

Throughout the legislative process, the president may attempt to persuade members of Congress to vote in support of bills that would further his or her agenda. One tactic the president uses to sway a legislator's vote is federal funds allocation. For example, a representative who provides the president with a key vote may in turn be granted finances to support a vital program for his or her constituents. When the president and congressional

President George W. Bush gives his 2007 State of the Union Address.

majorities are of the same political party, they can partner to deliver a unified agenda. Historically, this has rarely been the case, making presidential action another procedural check and balance.

Legislative Options

Traditionally, the enrolled act is signed first by the Speaker of the House and then by the president of the Senate (the vice president, if available, or the president pro tempore). After these signatures are obtained, the act returns to the chamber of its origin, where either the House clerk or secretary of the Senate presents the document to the White House. On receipt of the act by a White House clerk, the president has 10 days in which to take action. During this time, the president may have the act distributed to cabinet members who oversee related departments for their advisement.

If the president agrees with the act in its presented form, he may pass it into law simply by signing and dating the document. A messenger communicates the

President Lyndon Johnson signs into law the Civil Rights Act of 1964. The president plays an integral role in lawmaking; each law requires his or her signature before it is considered to be official.

news to the House and Senate chambers, and the signed document is delivered to the archivist of the United States, where the new law receives an official number. Laws are designated by their private or public status, the congressional session, and the order in which they passed. For example, the first public law passed in the 115th Congress was numbered *Public Law 115–1*, and the second was *Public Law 115–2*.

If the president disagrees with an enrolled act, he may refuse to sign it and instead veto the act or simply ignore it. A veto is a complete rejection of the act. Rather than signing the act into law, the president returns it to Congress with a veto message, which communicates the reasons why he or she did not sign the law. Often, the president is well aware of legislation under consideration in Congress, and if he or she disagrees with an act, Congress may be informed of plans for a presidential veto. This threat of veto can influence legislators to address the president's concerns prior to presenting the act.

An act vetoed by the president and retuned to Congress is not necessarily dead. Congress has the power to override a veto. If both chambers of Congress vote to accept the act by two-thirds majorities, the act becomes law without the president's signature. Then, the new law bypasses a second presidential action and is submitted to the archivist. If the act does not receive the required two-thirds majority in each chamber, however, it may be resubmitted for committee consideration to amend the sections disagreed with by the president. The act must be approved once again by both houses in identical form before resubmitting to the president.

If the president chooses to ignore an enrolled act, his or her inaction does not halt the process. By not taking direct action on a bill, the president is, in effect, passively taking action. From the time a White House clerk receives the act, the president has a 10-day deadline in which to either sign or veto the legislation. If the 10-day period expires before the president takes action, the act automatically becomes law without the president's signature. Typically, the president allows this to happen when he or she does not personally agree with the legislation, but the act has enough public support that vetoing it would reflect poorly on the president's popularity.

President Franklin D. Roosevelt vetoed 635 bills when he was in office.

LINE-ITEM VETO

For a brief period between 1997 and 1998, the president had an additional legislative option called the **line-item veto**. The line-item veto, which is used by many governors when addressing state legislation, enabled then-president Bill Clinton (1993–2001) to consider an act line by line and to cancel certain elements with which he did not agree. President Clinton would then sign the act into law and return the deleted sections to Congress, which could vote to overturn the president's decisions just as it would with a standard veto. The line-item veto, as defined, limited the president's power so that he could cancel only certain types of fiscal items.

The purpose of the line-item veto was to enable the president to eliminate region-specific (also known colloquially as *pork barrel*) benefits from national laws. President Clinton was the only president to employ the line-item veto, which he used 11 times during its existence to cancel 82 items. On June 25, 1998, in the case of *Clinton v. City of New York*, the U.S. Supreme Court ruled the line-item veto unconstitutional, thus eliminating the option. President George W. Bush attempted to reintroduce the line-item veto in 2006, but the proposed act was not approved by the Senate. It is interesting to note that in 1861, secessionists wrote similar presidential power into the Constitution of the Confederate States of America.

Unresolved bills do not carry over from one congressional session to the next, so an act received by the White House with fewer than 10 days remaining in the session is in a perilous position. Under those circumstances, if the president disagrees with the act, he can actually kill the legislation by taking no action—this is known as a **pocket veto**. The president does not sign the act. It is not vetoed, so Congress cannot override the decision, and as the session expires, the legislation dies. In order to submit an identical act, Congress must start from scratch during its next session.

Communication and Enforcement

Whether enacted into law by the president's signature, congressional override of a veto, or 10-day period expiration, the new law receives its official number from the archivist of the United States and is ready for publication. In an effort to communicate new laws as quickly and effectively as possible, the government publishes the legislation in three variations: **slip laws**, *The United States Statutes at Large*, and the United States Code. These formats are not direct channels to the general public, however, so we typically rely on the media, our local officials, or government resources such as the Library of Congress to follow legislative updates.

Prepared by the Office of the Federal Register, National Archives and Records Administration, within a few days of its enactment, the slip law is typically the first publication of a new law. The slip law is a document that contains the complete text of the law along with a comprehensive list of facts (including dates the bill passed in each chamber of Congress, which committees considered the legislation, and its inclusion in the *Congressional Record*) chronicling its legislative history. Copies of the slip law are available to officials and the public through the document rooms of either house of Congress, or directly from the Government Printing Office.

First printed in 1845, the *United States Statutes at Large* is a series of large, hardbound volumes that contains the full text of every law, public and private, ever

SIGNING STATEMENTS

During presidential action, when the president signs an act, he or she may attach a message known as a *signing statement*. Originally, the signing statement was designed to be a brief interpretation of the president's expected outcome of the law, an advisory note to the president's staff on enforcement, or a concern about the law's constitutionality. Any of these statements is valid; however, it is the judiciary's role to determine the constitutionality of our laws in practice. Things get tricky when the president believes a law to be unconstitutional and pledges in his signing statement not to enforce certain sections.

The signing statement was first used by President James Monroe (1817-1825). By 1980, only 75 total signing statements had been issued. Use and influence of these often-controversial notes have increased dramatically during recent administrations, however. Today, signing statements are added to a law's legislative history for consultation during judicial interpretation. President George W. Bush (2001–2009) personally issued more than 160 signing statements, identifying more than 1,000 challenges to provisions of the law. Signing statements, it seems, have replaced the line-item veto as a tactic for customizing laws to a president's demands.

The assistant chief of the Law Section of the Division of Research and Republication of the Department of State adds a new law into the Statutes at Large. *The* U.S. Statutes at Large *contain the full text of every law, public and private, ever passed by the U.S. government.*

passed by the U.S. government. At the end of each session of Congress, a new volume is added to the series, which includes all laws passed during the session, in the order in which they were enacted. When a new law is added to the *Statutes at Large*, its entry includes notes identifying precedent-setting legislation and cross references for simple location of relevant laws elsewhere in the *Statutes at Large*.

The *United States Code* contains all public laws in a condensed format, organized by title and section. This is the law resource used most frequently by officials who reference public laws on a daily basis. A new law is codified by the addition of numbers that refer to the corresponding title and section of the *U.S. Code*. These reference numbers then appear in the margins of the slip law and the *Statutes at Large*. The Office of the Law Revision Counsel of the House of Representatives publishes a new edition of the *U.S. Code* every six years, and a supplement featuring new laws passed during the term is released after each congressional session. In order to be effective, new laws must be simultaneously communicated to all levels of society. Judges who preside over the relevant area of law must become familiar enough with its text and history to interpret the law's intent and apply broad legislation to specific cases. Law enforcement agencies with jurisdiction over the particular law must be prepared to recognize an abuse of it and identify exactly which section of the *U.S. Code* is in violation, sometimes under highly stressful circumstances. Finally, the general public must be informed to know how to function within the boundaries of the law.

Upon enactment of a new federal law and communication through the various official channels, the law becomes the responsibility of the third branch of the U.S. government: the judiciary. The U.S. Supreme Court, the Courts of Appeals, and the

PUBLIC LAW CODES

Every public law is codified under one of the following categories:

Title 1	General Provisions
Title 2	The Congress
Title 3	The President
Title 4	Flag and Seal, Seat of Government, and the States
Title 5	Government Organization and Employees
Title 6	Domestic Security
Title 7	Agriculture
Title 8	Aliens and Nationality
Title 9	Arbitration
Title 10	Armed Forces
Title 11	Bankruptcy
Title 12	Banks and Banking
Title 13	Census
Title 14	Coast Guard
Title 15	Commerce and Trade
Title 16	Conservation
Title 17	Copyrights
Title 18	Crimes and Criminal Procedure

Title 19	Custom Duties
Title 20	Education
Title 21	Food and Drugs
Title 22	Foreign Relations and Intercourse
Title 23	Highways
Title 24	Hospitals and Asylums
Title 25	Indians
Title 26	Internal Revenue Code
Title 27	Intoxicating Liquors
Title 28	Judiciary and Judicial Procedure
Title 29	Labor
Title 30	Mineral Lands and Mining
Title 31	Money and Finance
Title 32	National Guard
Title 33	Navigation and Navigable Waters
Title 34	Navy (repealed)
Title 35	Patents
Title 36	Patriotic Societies and Observances
Title 37	Pay and Allowances of the Uniformed Services
Title 38	Veterans' Benefits
Title 39	Postal Service
Title 40	Public Buildings, Property, and Works
Title 41	Public Contracts
Title 42	The Public Health and Welfare
Title 43	Public Lands
Title 44	Public Printing and Documents
Title 45	Railroads
Title 46	Shipping
Title 47	Telegraphs, Telephones, and Radiotelegraphs
Title 48	Territories and Insular Possessions
Title 49	Transportation
Title 50	War and National Defense

Above is a view of the U.S. Supreme Court Building, where the eight associate justices and the chief justice conduct their day-to-day business. The Supreme Court has an important role regarding the law—when a law is challenged, it is up to the Court to determine whether the law at issue is constitutional.

District Courts have jurisdiction over federal laws. Judges who preside over these courts must be nominated by the president and confirmed by the Senate. The courts interpret laws based on constitutionality, but judges continually apply new thinking and precedent-setting legislation to interpret laws based on the standards of the day. A law may be changed or repealed only through the legislative process. But the Supreme Court may strike down a law if it deems it unconstitutional.

Conclusion

Existing laws are constantly challenged by the changing times, from shifting public priorities to emerging technologies. Music copyright laws are a perfect example. Congress passed its first music copyright laws in the 1800s—prior to the existence of the recording industry—to protect songwriters' rights to sheet music. The recording industry emerged in the twentieth century, and copyright laws evolved to take into consideration recorded music for purchase and broadcast. Today, in the twenty-first century, Congress struggles to adapt music copyright laws to a landscape encompassing everything from digital downloads to satellite radio to ringtones for your phone.

The U.S. government's procedure for creating, amending, and passing new laws, however, remains constant. When the process is respected and adhered to by all parties, it is a near-flawless system: checks and balances across three branches of government; equal representation of the people, with opportunities for participation by engaged citizens; meticulous consideration and spirited debate over new legislation; and a Constitution against which to appraise new laws as they apply to specific situations. The process has been sturdy enough to serve as our country's cornerstone for more than two centuries and is flexible enough to carry us confidently into the future.

Text-Dependent Questions

1. What does the president's State of the Union Address usually include?
2. Explain the difference between a line-item veto and a pocket veto.
3. How often does the Office of the Law Revision Counsel of the House of Representatives publish a new edition of the *U.S. Code*?

Research Project

Research a U.S. president who used the veto. Write a brief report including notable vetoes, the historical circumstances around their use, and their political and legal consequences. Bonus: Research a second president from a different era of U.S. history and his use of the veto. Can any conclusions be drawn about the way the use of the veto has changed over time?

Series Glossary of Key Terms

Abolitionist: A person committed to abolishing a certain practice, such as slavery or unfair criminal justice practices.

Acquittal: When a person is cleared of a charge of an offense.

Ambassador: A person who acts as the representative of a nation, organization, or other group in discussions or negotiations with others.

Amnesty: To give an official pardon to a person accused of an offense.

Appeal: In legal terms, to apply to a higher court to review, and possibly overturn, the decision of a lower court.

Apportionment: The division of something, such as money, among a group.

Bicameral: Used to describe a legislative body with two chambers.

Bond: A type of financial instrument in which the issuer agrees to repay an investor a certain amount of money with interest over time.

Cabinet: In government, a group of advisers of a head of state.

Canvass: To appeal directly to people in hopes of securing their votes.

Casework: Assistance in matters of government provided by a senator to a constituent, including answering questions, explaining policies, or determining eligibility.

Caucus: A gathering of members of a specific political party or organization to form policy positions, choose leaders, and make other decisions relevant to the organization.

Censure: To formally and publicly express disapproval of a person or action.

Census: An official count of a population, often including other data or information about that population.

Centrist: A politician who favors policies that are neither too liberal nor too conservative.

Chief justice: The highest ranking judge on a court with multiple judges; in the United States, the head of the Supreme Court.

Civil service: The professional public sector of a government (not including the military, judicial branches, or elected officials), staffed by people who are hired for their skills rather than elected or appointed.

Cloture: A means of ending debate on a bill in order to force a vote.

Common law: Laws based on past custom, or what has been judged over time to be lawful or unlawful.

Conference committee: In the U.S. Congress, a temporary committee made up of both House and Senate members, organized to prepare a version of an act that incorporates amendments from both chambers.

Constituent: A person who can vote and is represented by a public official.

Decentralized: Used to describe a system in which power is dispersed among people, states, or other entities, rather than controlled by one administrative body.

Deficit spending: When a government spends money that it has borrowed rather than collected through taxes.

Delegate: A person dispatched to represent others at a conference, legislative session, or other official event.

Demographic: A specific part of a population.

Deposition: Testimony taken down in writing.

Diplomat: An official representative of one country to another.

Duty: A tax or fee placed on imported or exported goods.

Egalitarian: Of or related to the belief that humans are equal, especially with respect to social, political, and economic rights and privileges.

Electoral College: A body of representatives from each state, who formally vote to elect the president and vice president.

Excise tax: A tax on a specific good or activity, often included in the overall price.

Executive branch: The U.S. government entity that enforces laws, with the president at its head.

Extrajudicial: Describing an act that is not legally authorized.

Federal deficit: The amount of money the federal government spends in excess of what it collects in taxes.

Federalist: An advocate of a central national government that unites states and leaves various powers to state governments.

Filibuster: The strategy of legislators talking indefinitely to prevent a vote on a bill.

Franchise: An individual's right to vote.

Gold standard: A monetary system where the value of currency is based on a specific quantity of gold.

Habeas corpus: A legal means by which a person can contest unlawful imprisonment; the term is Latin for "You have the body."

Impeachment: A charge of wrongdoing or misconduct against a public official that may result in termination from office.

Inaugurate: To begin a policy or practice; to formally admit someone into a public office.

Incumbent: A person currently holding a political office.

Indict: To formally charge someone of a crime.

Isolationist: A policy that favors limited or no engagement in international affairs.

Legislature: The assembly of a government or state that is tasked with making laws.

Libertarian: A person who believes completely in the free will and choice of individuals.

Line-item veto: The power of a chief executive to reject certain parts of a bill.

Lobbyist: A person who advocates for particular policies or positions.

Mandate: An instruction to do something in a certain way.

Motion: A formal proposal or request put before a legislative body.

Naturalization: The process of granting a person from one country citizenship of another country.

Originalism: When referring to the U.S. Constitution, a belief that the document should be interpreted along the lines of the Framers' original intent.

Pardon: To release someone of all punishments for a crime.

Parliamentarian: A person who advises a legislative body on matters of procedure.

Partisanship: Strong adherence to a particular cause or group, often at the expense of compromise with others.

Perjury: An act of lying under oath.

Platform: A set of policy goals on which a candidate bases a campaign.

Pocket veto: When a president indirectly vetoes a bill by leaving it unsigned as a legislative session expires.

Political action committee: An organization that raises funds to influence elections, ballot measures, or other legislation.

Polling: In politics, soliciting the opinions of the public to help determine electoral preferences.

Primary: An election within a political party to choose its candidates for a race.

Progressive: In political science, a person who seeks to advance society through implementation of new policies and ideas.

Pro tempore: A Latin phrase meaning "for the time being," used to describe when a person holds a position in the absence of a superior.

Provision: A requirement, restriction, or condition set forth in a legal document.

Quorum: The minimum number of members of a group who need to be present in order to officially conduct business.

Recession: A period of economic decline, with drops in both trade and production of goods.

Reprieve: To grant a delay in sentencing for a crime.

Resolution: A formal proposal adopted by a governing body.

Secession: The formal withdrawal from a state, alliance, or other political body.

Slip law: A document containing the complete text of a new law along with its legislative history, often the law's first published form.

Subpoena: A formal document ordering someone to provide evidence or testimony, most often to a court.

Subsidized: Funded by an outside source.

Suffragist: A person who advocates for others' right to vote.

Supermajority: A vote total that represents significantly more than one-half of the voting assembly, often 60 percent or two-thirds.

Tariff: A tax on imported or exported goods.

Treason: An act of betraying one's country.

Veto: The power to reject a legislative bill and refuse to sign it into law.

Further Reading & Internet Resources

BOOKS

***House and Senate.* 4th ed.** By Ross K. Baker. Published in 2008 by W.W. Norton, New York. Drawing on interviews with legislators, this book presents a complete portrait of the bicameral U.S. Congress.

***Unorthodox Lawmaking: New Legislative Processes in the U.S. Congress.* 5th ed.** Published in 2016 by CQ Press, Washington, D.C. A comprehensive look at the complex procedures and protocols of the U.S. Congress, including how these working methods came to be and the ways they influence legislation.

Master of the Senate: The Years of Lyndon Johnson. By Robert Caro. Published in 2002 by Vintage, New York. The third volume of historian Robert Caro's expansive biography of Lyndon Johnson covers Johnson's years in the Senate, where he became a powerful majority leader and oversaw the passage of the Civil Rights Act of 1957.

Congress and Policy Making in the 21st Century. Edited by Jeffrey A. Jenkins and Eric P. Patashnik. Published in 2016 by Cambridge University Press, New York. This collection of essays examines different perspectives on the role, power, and function of Congress in the 21st century, focusing on key policy issues such as rising income inequality, health care, and immigration.

WEB SITES

The Library of Congress. http://www.loc.gov. Visit the online home of the Library of Congress to search troves of digital records, from historical photographs to presidential papers to audio recordings.

U.S. Government Printing Office. http://www.gpo.gov. Learn about how the Government Printing Office keeps America informed, by visiting its Web site containing information about its history, current news and media, and a special section for students and educators.

U.S. House of Representatives. http://www.house.gov. The official site of the U.S. House features information on individual representatives, current legislation, and Congressional committees.

U.S. Senate. http://www.senate.gov. The expansive site of the U.S. Senate provides information on individual senators, current legislative calendars, and even the paintings and sculptures decorating the Senate.

The Supreme Court is the final arbiter of whether a law is constitutional.

Index

A

acts, 55–56
amendments, 62, 64–66

B

bills, 22–32, 35–43
branches of government, 10, 13

C

Capitol Building, 15
census, 10, 12
Civil War, 7
committees
  hearings before, 36–40
  legislative consideration by, 34–35
  reports by, 40–43
Congress, 6
  bills introduced to, 44–46, 54–62
  committees of, 17–21, 29–32, 35–43
  duties of, 14, 22–24
  laws enacted by, 62, 64–74
  legislative calendar, 57–59
  organization of, 10–21
Congressional Record, 29, 61, 72
Constitution, 10, 12, 23

E

elections, 14, 16

F

federal agencies, 8–10
federalism, 6–9
filibuster, 54, 61

H

Hamilton, Alexander, 6
House of Representatives
  committees of, 14
  and conference committee, 68–71
  duties of, 14
  floor of, 48–49
  legislative role of, 26–28, 44–46, 64–68
  size of, 11–12
  term limits in, 14
  voting process, 49–53

J

Jackson, Andrew, 7
Jefferson, Thomas, 32, 54

L

legislative process, 17–23, 62
  and committees, 34–43, 68–74
  Congress and, 26–29
  and enacted laws, 78–87
  legislative calendar, 42
  legislative day, 56–57
  origin of bills in, 24–26
  role of president in, 76–77
  within House of Representatives, 44–53
  within Senate, 54–62
  See also House of Representatives; Senate
lobbyists, 24

M

Manual of Parliamentary Practice, 54

N

New Deal, 8

P

president pro tempore, 16, 29, 55
presidential action, 77–84
presiding officer, 16, 57–58, 61
public law codes, 85–86

Q

QR Video
  Barack Obama veto, 77
  committee hearing, 37
  Congressional Record, 71
  House floor footage, 50
  legislative branch, 12
  legislative process, 24
  Senate floor footage, 61
quorum, 44, 50

S

Senate
  bill considerations by, 54, 56–57
  chamber of, 57–60
  and conference committee, 68–71
  debates within, 60–62
  duties of, 14
  and filibuster, 61
  legislative calendar of, 57–59
  legislative role of, 26–28, 44–46
  size of, 11, 15
  term limits in, 14
separation of powers, 6–7
Speaker of the House, 14
spoils system, 7–8
State of the Union address, 76–77

T

two-party system, 16

V

veto, 77, 79, 81
vice-president, 16

W

Washington, D.C., 15
Washington, George, 6

Credits

COVER

(clockwise from top left) Stephanie Chasez/U.S. Department of Defense; U.S. Senate; Everett Historical/Shutterstock; Mark Reinstein/Shutterstock

INTERIOR

1, J Main/Shutterstock; 11, BigFishDesign/iStock; 13, JPLDesigns/iStock; 15, Lunamarina/Dreamstime; 17, United States Senate/Wikimedia Commons; 20 (UP), Wellesenterprises/Wikimedia Commons; 20 (LO), Wellesenterprises/Wikimedia Commons; 23, Pgiam/iStock; 25, magnez2/iStock; 28, United States Congress/Wikimedia Commons; 30, Library of Congress/Wikimedia Commons; 31, National Portrait Gallery, Smithsonian Institution/Wikimedia Commons; 35, Joe Sohm/Dreamstime; 37, American Press Association/Wikimedia Commons; 40, Scott J. Ferrell/Newscom; 42, matt_benoit/iStock; 45, Georgesheldon/Dreamstime; 47, Paula Maxheim/Dreamstime; 49, USCapitol/Flickr; 51, Library of Congress; 52, Pete Marovich/Newscom; 55, Joe Sohm/Dreamstime; 57, Library of Congress; 58, Stuart Monk/Dreamstime; 60, The White House/Wikimedia Commons; 62, Chine Nouvelle/Newscom; 65, Jon Bilous/Dreamstime; 67, Library of Congress; 70, Vlad G/Shutterstock; 72, United States Congress/Wikimedia Commons; 73, Tom Williams/Newscom; 77, The White House/Wikimedia Commons; 78, Cecil Stoughton, White House Press Office/Wikimedia Commons; 80, Wikimedia Commons; 83, Harris & Ewing Photographs/Library of Congress; 84, Konstantin Lobastov/Dreamstime